D0846648

Reflect
&Write

300 POEMS AND PHOTOGRAPHS TO INSPIRE WRITING

Reflect &Write

COMPILED BY
ELIZABETH GUY AND HANK KELLNER

PRUFROCK PRESS INC.
WACO, TEXAS

PHOTOGRAPH CREDITS: All of the photos in this work are by Hank Kellner except for those found on the following pages:
31 lower left, 31 lower right, 45 upper left, 45 upper right, 45 lower left, 55, 64, 78, 84, 99, 101,
127, 137, 141, 145 courtesy Cynthia Lee Katona
33 courtesy Timothy San Pedro
35 illustration courtesy Jennifer Bowles
36, 37, 93, 96, 106, 138 courtesy Laura Pastuszek
47 *Der Schrei der Natur* (*The Scream of Nature*) by Edvard Munch, 1893
49, 60 lower right, 131 courtesy Molly Bennett
50 courtesy Kym Sheehan
54, 120 courtesy Michele Kelley
56 courtesy Martha Walker
61 courtesy Cindy Nadal
69, 83 courtesy Anna Kellner
81 lower right courtesy David Kellner
86 courtesy Elizabeth V. Best
114 courtesy Taylor Dennehy
125 courtesy Mary Meyer
126, 130 courtesy Elizabeth Guy
133, 140, 142 courtesy Paul Stubbs

Copyright ©2013 Prufrock Press Inc.

Edited by Sean Redmond

Production design by Raquel Trevino

ISBN-13: 978-1-61821-023-4

At the time of this book's publication, all facts and figures cited are the most current available; all telephone numbers, addresses, and website URLs are accurate and active; all publications, organizations, websites, and other resources exist as described in this book; and all have been verified. The authors and Prufrock Press make no warranty or guarantee concerning the information and materials given out by organizations or content found at websites, and we are not responsible for any changes that occur after this book's publication. If you find an error or believe that a resource listed here is not as described, please contact Prufrock Press.

Prufrock Press Inc.
P.O. Box 8813
Waco, TX 76714-8813
Phone: (800) 998-2208
Fax: (800) 240-0333
http://www.prufrock.com

Table of Contents

Foreword

This arrangement of poignant poems, vital pictures, and compelling quotations from such literary giants as Wordsworth and Voltaire is so beautifully crafted that I hesitate to offer an introduction. This work is obviously the creation of many accomplished writers who know how to inspire others to create poetry as well as prose. For that reason, my words of praise feel leaden and inadequate.

I know from my own classroom experience the power of the visual to evoke meaningful writing. When the provocative and often delicate poems in *Reflect and Write* are paired with perfectly selected artwork and accompanied by thoughtful quotations from a diverse range of wonderful thinkers, success is inevitable.

Even for professionals, writing can be difficult. Because it can be like opening a vein, we need to offer the best incentives and inspiration possible and in that way ensure that our students will respond positively. Wise teachers who plumb this book's depth will find great success in doing so, just as night follows day.

Joe Milner, Ph.D.
Professor of English education
Wake Forest University

Introduction

Reflect and Write presents a collection of more than 300 poems and black and white photographs created by 26 students, 23 teachers, and 12 other writers and photographers nationwide. Each page includes a poem and a photograph as well as a related quotation and four keywords. Many of the poems also include either an Inspiration 💡 or Challenge ◎ prompt. The Inspiration prompts are designed to help your students start thinking about the poem from a critical perspective. The Challenge prompts can be used to help students complete written works of their own. Together, these materials are sure to foster spirited class discussion and interesting and exciting written works. No longer will students complain that they "don't know what to write about!"

Before bringing the book into the classroom, teachers should take time to look over the "12 Ways to Inspire Your Students" section. Here, they will find suggestions for teacher-directed activities that can help students overcome their reluctance to write and improve their critical thinking and writing skills. The "Themes to Explore" section provides suggested poems for use by theme along with a list of all student-written poems, and the "Internet Resources" section includes two listings of websites that provide information, tips, and resources regarding student publishing.

Each page of the book allows for flexibility in its use. Some students may choose to respond only to a poem or a quotation as they seek inspiration for their writing. Others may consider a combination of a poem and a photo. Still others will respond to other combinations of the words and images found in this collection. Also note that student-written poems are identified by the ✏ symbol. Some students may become more enthusiastic when reading work written by their peers, and therefore these poems have been identified accordingly.

The possibilities for using poems, photographs, quotations, and keywords as motivation for discussion and writing are almost endless. Our hope is that *Reflect and Write* will inspire students to use their imaginations and help them to develop the communication and critical thinking skills necessary for success in today's world.

We would like to thank the students and teachers at the following schools for their generous contributions to the work: Allen County Scottsville High School, Scottsville, KY; Arizona State University, Tempe, AZ; Beacon High School, Newton, MA; Bel Air High School, Bel Air, MD; Bolingbrook High School, Bolingbrook, IL; Butler Community College, Wichita, KS; Calloway County

High School, Murray, KY; Capital High School, Charleston, WV; Central High School, St. Joseph, MO; Charlotte County Public Schools, Port Charlotte, FL; CICS Northtown Academy, Chicago, IL; Clay Elementary School, Clay, KY; D.J. "Red" Simon Middle School, Kyle, TX; Glenbard South High School, Glen Ellyn, IL; Greenville Elementary School; Greenville, KY; Horizon High School, Scottsdale, AZ; Lake Forest High School, Lake Forest, IL; Lincoln-Way Central High School, New Lenox, IL; Minooka Community High School, Channahon, IL; Missouri Western State University, St. Joseph, MO; Muhlenberg South Elementary School, Belton, KY; Ohlone College, Fremont, CA; Park Day School, Oakland, CA; Peak to Peak Charter School, Lafayette, CO; Round Rock Opportunity Center, Round Rock, TX; Stanberry R-II School District, Stanberry, MO; Stony Point High School, Round Rock, TX; Sunshine Elementary School, Lehigh Acres, FL; Weston Middle School, Weston, CT; and Westport Middle School, Louisville, KY. We also give thanks to the many other contributors who have provided either poetry and/or photography to this collection, including Cynthia Lee Katona, who lent us extensive use of her photographs and haiku. You can read more of her haiku in the collection *Maybe...and That's Final* (Blurb, 2011) and access her portfolio at http://www.photomerchant.com. And we would be remiss if we did not thank our editor, Sean Redmond, for the skill he demonstrated in editing our manuscript.

We would also like to take this time to note that a portion of the proceeds from the sale of this book will be donated to the Wounded Warrior Project.

Elizabeth Guy
Hank Kellner

12 Ways to Inspire Your Students

1. **USE YOUR HAIKU**

   This collection contains 24 haiku, to be found on various "Four Haiku" pages. During class discussion, point out that these poems use few words to create an image in the reader's mind. Indicate that traditional haiku contain three lines of five, seven, and five syllables each (though this is not a hard and fast rule, and some haiku in this collection do not adhere to it). Then direct your students to select any of the photographs in the book as inspiration for writing their own haiku. Stress the need for brevity and the careful choice of words.

2. **GENEALOGICAL STUDY**

   "Where I'm From" (p. 25) and "From the Love of My Parents" (p. 54) are two poems in which the authors describe their origins. After discussing the poems, have your students interview older members of their families to discover more about their own backgrounds. Then direct the students to use the information they have discovered to write poems of their own based on their findings. Ask them to include family photographs with their work whenever possible.

3. **EXPLORATION OF THEMES**

   Divide the class into three or four groups and distribute photocopies of several different pages from this collection to each group. Direct the students to exchange ideas about the themes of the poems, and have each group come up with a list. Then ask them to develop their own works based on the themes they have cited. As a follow-up activity, students may read their creations to their classmates and have their classmates try to correctly identify the chosen theme. (For a list of suggested themes and corresponding poems, see "Themes to Explore" immediately following this section.)

4. **QUESTIONS, QUESTIONS**

   "Not Me!" (p. 67), "Where Is My Heart?" (p. 104), and "A Forever's Goodbye " (p. 128) are three examples of poems in this collection that involve questions. After discussing the poems with your students, direct them to write one or more questions about any topic on a sheet of paper. Collect the papers, shuffle them, and distribute them to the class. Direct the students to compose poems of at least three stanzas or brief essays in response to the questions.

5. **RAP IT UP**

   Many students are familiar with rap, a form of poetry in which the words are spoken to the accompaniment of a set rhythm or beat. Choose a poem from this collection and analyze it for poetic devices such as simile, metaphor, symbolism, and personification. Then have students try to fit the poem to a rap. Afterward, students can write their own rap compositions using the poetic techniques they studied. Finally, conduct a poetry slam in which students may volunteer to read their creations to the class.

6. **COMPILE AN ANTHOLOGY**

   Select any poem-photo combination in this collection and discuss it with your class in terms of its relationship to the quotation and keywords that accompany it. Direct your students to select images from any source to use as inspiration for their own writing. Then have them find appropriate quotations and keywords to add to their compositions. Finally, compile a class anthology using the students' combinations of photos, poems, keywords, and quotations.

7. **GET BACK TO NATURE**

   Read "winter's here," (p. 23), "The Last Day" (p. 44), "Approaching Autumn" (p. 51), "Self-Identification in the Crinkling of Fall" (p. 99), and other appropriate poems and discuss how the poets use nature to support their themes. Then ask your students to set up four headings titled Spring, Summer, Fall, and Winter. Direct them to list appropriate descriptions under each heading. These descriptions may take the form of sense impressions, similes, or metaphors. During class discussion, create a master list of all of the students' responses, and direct them to write poems related to nature using items of their choice from the list.

8. **COMPARE . . .**

   Conduct a class discussion in which you discuss the use of comparison as a form of rhetoric in any appropriate poem in this collection. For example, in Betty Bowman's "Walls" (p. 79), the author compares walls to problems we encounter in our lives. In "Butterflies" (p. 91), Cole Kim compares passing years to butterflies. Encourage the students to think of unlikely, insightful, beautiful, or just plain bizarre comparisons. You can also have students think of objects independently, then pair them up and challenge them to find ways in which their different objects are similar.

9. **. . . AND CONTRAST**
In William Shakespeare's "Sonnet 18" (p. 52), the poet glorifies the person about whom he writes. By contrast, in "Sonnet 18.5" (p. 52), Hank Kellner criticizes his subject. After you discuss these poems with your students, ask them to write brief pieces about a teacher, friend, or family member in which they present contrasting descriptions of their subjects.

10. **POINTS OF VIEW**
In the first and second stanzas of "Summer Storms" (p. 64), the author vividly describes an event that took place years earlier when she and another young person experienced a storm. Speaking in the first person, she writes: "As we peered past drawn curtains,/The storm seemed unending." But after the storm passed, the two frightened children emerged into "golden light" in which they "played until sunset." Ask your students to use the first person point of view to write poems or other compositions in which they recall certain memories. Experiment with writing about the same events from different points of view.

11. **ALLITERATION**
Reading poems solely for the pleasure of their sounds is one of the ways teachers can help students think about the sound of their words while writing. In Rachel Penn's "Lily Loves the Lantern Man" (p. 63), the author repeats the sound of the letter "L" to create an aural impression. In Kristel Greenlove's "I Love a Parade" (p. 30), Greenlove uses alliteration when describing "The brilliant blare of the sounding brass." After discussing the concept, have students look for alliteration in the world around them: in newspapers, in advertisements, on the Internet. Have students bring in these found phrases and combine them to form poems or use them as inspiration to create new poems of their own.

12. **REPETITION**
"Where I'm From" (p. 25), "Letter to Urban Youth" (p. 34), "The Kiss I Got From You" (p. 43), and "Time" (p. 75) use the repetition of certain words, phrases, or clauses as a way to emphasize the poems' main ideas. Read these poems to your students, and ask them to pay close attention to the poets' use of repetition. Then direct your students to emulate this technique in brief poems or other compositions. Make sure to have them analyze the different effects this technique can produce.

Themes to Explore

Following are some of the themes covered in this collection of poems. The listings are not comprehensive but should prove a good starting point for teachers who wish to focus on certain topics or ideas. The title of the poem and its page number are listed.

Students ages 9–18 provided many of the poems in this book. Seeing fellow students' writing in print can be particularly inspiring, and therefore we've compiled a list indicating which poems are student-written for your convenience. On the pages that these poems appear, you will also see this symbol ✎ indicating the poem on that page is a student composition.

Internet Resources

The Internet is a wonderful tool, and it can help both teachers and students. It's a great source of resources to help teach the art of writing, and there are many websites that assist with lesson planning, providing classroom ideas and advice. You can find access to many poems and other writings that might not be available in the school library, as well as photos and other materials for inspiration. It's also an invaluable tool for helping your students get published. Below, find two lists of websites that can help you to augment the activities in this book.

10 Websites to Help Teachers in the Classroom

http://www.poets.org

This website is operated by the Academy of American Poets, a nonprofit organization that supports American poets at all stages of their careers and fosters an appreciation of contemporary poetry. Its website has information specifically for educators, broken into the following sections: Tips for Teaching Poetry, Poetry Resources for Teens, Curriculum and Lesson Plans, Great Poems to Teach, Essays on Teaching, Teaching Resource Center, and Poetry Read-a-Thon.

http://www.poetryforge.org

The University of Virginia hosts this open source archive designed to allow teachers and student writers to explore open source writing tools in the English classroom. Sections include Teaching with Poetry Tools, Resources, and a gallery that showcases student and teacher writing.

http://www.poetryfoundation.org/learning

The Poetry Foundation's Learning Lab offers annotated poems, guides to poems, articles for teachers, and teacher tips, as well as discussions, questions, and writing prompts for students. It also includes a glossary of poetic terms and a collection of essays on poetic theory. The Poetry Foundation's online archive consists of 11,000 poems by 3,000 poets.

http://www.readwritethink.org

Created by the International Reading Association and the National Council of Teachers of English, this website contains lesson plans, student interactive activities for students, mobile apps, calendar activities, and printouts related to reading and writing. Teachers can also contribute classroom-related activities to this site.

http://www.twc.org
Based in New York City, the Teachers & Writers Collaborative (T&W) "seeks to educate the imagination by offering innovative creative writing programs for students and teachers." Resources offered include lesson plans and sample materials, a blog, and links to organizations that work with teachers worldwide. T&W also publishes *Teachers & Writers* magazine and conducts workshops in the New York City area.

http://www.creativity-portal.com
This website is home to an online community that inspires creativity through personal expression and the arts. It features articles, photos, and illustrations by writers and others willing to share ideas. The organization publishes a monthly newsletter/e-zine.

http://www.webenglishteacher.com
Operated by English teacher Carla Beard, this website is the equivalent of an online faculty library/faculty workroom. It contains lesson plans, articles, and valuable information at every level and in every area of teaching English, including AP and IB, drama, grammar, journalism, literature, media, and more. It also offers videos, e-texts, suggestions for technology integration, and classroom activities, and it publishes a free newsletter.

http://merlynspen.org
Merlyn's Pen hosts the New Library of Young Adult Writing, an extensive collection of published fiction, poetry, and personal essays written by students. It offers lesson plans and activities to help teach writing, as well as a Teacher Bulletin Board section and more than 1,000 writing models. Its special collections focus on humor writing, writing about nature and the sea, and coming of age poems and stories.

http://www.starteaching.com
Frank Holes's StarTeaching website features tips, techniques, lesson plans, writing prompts, activities, and articles for teachers. It contains special reports on technology, administration, concepts, skills, planning, requirements, benchmarks, integration, writing across the curriculum, and more information about education. Its extensive lists of writing prompts are particularly helpful.

http://www.nwp.org

The National Writing Project hosts a network of 200 local sites anchored at colleges and universities, serving teachers at all levels, early childhood through university. This organization is working to create a future where every person is an accomplished writer, engaged learner, and active participant in a digital, interconnected world. It offers high-quality professional development programs for educators.

10 Websites to Help Students Get Published

Students looking to submit work to the following publications should visit these websites and study each publication's submission guidelines carefully before doing so.

http://www.teenink.com

Teen Ink publishes online poetry, fiction, nonfiction, reviews, and art/photography created by teens ages 13–19. It hosts forums as well as a college guide that contains top college essays from around the country. This organization also publishes a magazine and books, all of which are dedicated solely to teens' work.

http://www.hanginloosepress.org

Hanging Loose magazine was first published in 1966, and it's one of the oldest independent literary magazines in the country. A section of each issue is devoted to high school writers, who are encouraged to submit poetry or short stories. A small monetary award and two copies of the issue are given to all accepted writers. In addition to the magazine, Hanging Loose Press has published four anthologies of work by high school students.

http://www.theclaremontreview.ca

The Claremont Review is a Canadian magazine that showcases the works of young adult writers, ages 13–19. It publishes poetry, fiction, drama, and art, and has accepted submissions from teenagers all over the world. It also sponsors an annual writing contest. *The Claremont Review* is issued twice yearly and distributed across Canada, but can be ordered by bookstores or directly from the website.

http://www.writingconference.com/writer's.htm

The Writers' Slate publishes original poetry and prose from students in grades K–12. It also publishes pedagogical and creative writing by teachers. Three issues per year are published online, with one issue devoted to publishing the winners of its writing contests.

http://www.polyphonyhs.com

Polyphony H.S. is a professional-quality literary magazine written, edited, and published by high school students. The organization's goal is to build strong writer-editor relationships and foster a community devoted to improving students' literary skills. It focuses on poetry, fiction, and creative nonfiction. It also cosponsors the Claudia Ann Seaman Awards competition, open to students in grades 9–12, which offers cash prizes of $200.

http://www.youngwritersmagazine.com

Young Writers magazine (formerly known as *Frodo's Notebook*) is an independent online publication committed to showcasing young writers' work. In addition to publishing art, literature, and literary criticism of 13–19 year olds, this organization also works to connect young writers to adults who work in writing and publishing, including professional writers, college professors, and others. This website also offers tips for teen writers.

http://artandwriting.org

The Alliance for Young Artists & Writers presents the Scholastic Art & Writing Awards, the longest-running recognition program for teenage creativity in the US. Former winners include Andy Warhol, Sylvia Plath, Joyce Carol Oates, and Truman Capote, among others. This organization works with more than 100 regional programs to help students from local communities participate; students in grades 7–12 are eligible. This program offers the largest source of scholarship funding for young artists and writers in the country. Publications include the *National Catalog of The Scholastic Art & Writing Awards*, published annually, as well as The Best Teen Writing annual anthology series and *Spark,* which publishes works by students in grades 7 and 8.

http://www.louisvillereview.org

The Louisville Review is a literary magazine housed at Spalding University in Louisville, KY. Each issue of the magazine contains a section called The Children's Corner, which focuses on poetry from students in grades K–12. Students should be aware that this publication looks especially for pieces that offer "fresh ways to recreate scenes and feelings," and is interested more in emotions and imagery than in rhyme scheme or moral or philosophical contemplation.

http://figment.com

Figment is a website devoted to teen writing and YA literature. Visitors can share their own stories, connect with other readers, and discover new authors. There are many writing contests that students can enter, along with forums for discussion, a blog, and a section for educators.

http://teenswritingforteens.co.nr

Teens Writing for Teens is a website dedicated to helping teen writers hone their craft and get published. It provides links to publications that specialize in teen writing (many of which also appear on this list), as well as advice and suggested reading. Its blog offers book reviews, and teen writers can submit book reviews of their own for publication.

Poems

Please note: While the vast majority of poems in this collection are suitable for students of all ages, a few present topics that teachers may find too mature for classrooms with younger students. As such, we recommend that teachers review the poems before use and ensure that they are appropriate for their students and communities.

reflections on the water's surface

by Sarah Marlin

A pebble
seen through the water's eyes,
disfigured,
its image rippling.
A toss,
a silent splash.
Something so
powerless,
small,
makes such a big
impact.
Its image,
crafted on the water's surface,
a movement in the still water,
shattering the cool surface of the
     shimmering lake.
You wave,
And your reflection waves back.
This person you see in the rippling
     water is
Distorted.
Changed.

In what ways have you observed changes in yourself, a family member, or someone you know? Describe both the physical and emotional aspects of these changes.

*"Only in quiet waters do things mirror themselves undistorted. Only in a quiet
mind is adequate perception of the world."*   —Hans Margolius

Keywords: Image   Reflections   Distortion   Shimmer

Molten Glass

by Betty Bowman

Colors swirl and melt
Into muted shapes
That have no meaning,
No clear shape fixes them
To things my eyes can recognize.

Blue, black, subtle green,
Too muted to be seen,
The liquid shapes
Melt into molten glass.
Like gentle waves
On a moonlit lake.

But when, as if by magic,
The water seems to slow its pace
As if to take a breath,
I can see the very things
That once eluded me.

Ah, there's a moment long forgotten,
And there's a long lost love.
And there's the time when I . . .
And another when I . . .

But why this yearning for the past?
Those times are gone.
Like breezes on a summer night
Or yesterday's sunset.

And tomorrow's still to come.

So I will live my life each day
As if it were my last.
And fondly bid *adieu*
To days that are long past.

Think of several events in the past that have affected your life, and consider how these events might affect your future.

"Carpe Diem." —Horace

Keywords: Color   Glass   Liquid   Flow

Little Girl, Little Girl

by Hillary Lockhart

Little girl, little girl
Tell me, what do you want to be?

I want be a doctor, lawyer, or an airplane
    pilot
to fly high above the trees.

Little girl, little girl
Tell me, what do you want to be?

Mother, teacher, mayor,
Oh yeah, drive a bright red fire truck,
    and be a fire chief.

Little girl, little girl
Tell me, what do you want to be?

I want to be an astronaut so I can soar to
    the moon
and sprinkle my dreams among the stars.

I want to be a beautiful
African Queen like magnificent Nefertiti.

I want to be a famous architect, and build towering
    skyscrapers;
or I can be a police woman—keep my city safe,
and protect all the little children in my hood.

Little girl, little girl
Tell me, what do you want to be?

Tell you the truth
I just want to read like the little girl that sits next to
    me.

Teacher brags how smart she is and I want to read
so everybody be proud of me.
I like to be a nurse, scientist, or even invent.
If you teach me to write and read, I can believe in
    my dreams.
`Cause an education can open the doors closed in
    my life.
I'll be able to protect myself; drive granny to the
    doctor and store.
Surely I can be my brother and sister's role model.
I gotta read and be something special!

The teacher reached out and grasped her hand
and softly hummed, "Little girl, little girl
walk with me. I'll teach you how to write and read."

"Books . . . .if you're going to be anything, they are vital in life." —Roald Dahl

Keywords: Doors   Dreams   Reading   Profession

Why I Write
(Adapted from the poem "Why I Write" by Tim Swain)

by Lisa Blair

Ask me why I write.

I dibbled and dabbled,
But none were
Quite the same as home.

Lucky.
Excuse me while I steal the sky;
Recapture my youth;
Make sense of life;
Sing so angelic;

Breathe soul into an education.

I write
Expressions of my individualism.
The eye, and the heart.

Fear.
Love.
Believe.

I cry at night.

I cry with my voice.
I cry with my pen.

I cry ink and tears and screams
Of fear and joy.

Ask me
Why
I
Write!

"Fill your paper with the breathings of your heart." —William Wordsworth

Keywords: Imagination   Author   Reveal   Memoir

Soda Shop Stop

by Anna Catherine

It was a small soda shop
in a small little town
where we'd stopped to watch a fair—
a festival scene
on a grassy green—
a party in ginger-ale air.

In that small soda shop
with its bent iron chairs
sitting outside by the door
we stopped
in the heat of the moment
to rest a moment or more.

In the heat of the moment
we stopped
to share a cone
of chocolate ice cream
mounded round as a dream
and dripping its own
tongue-licking cool cream.

Which I licked with you,
making swirls of my own
with my tongue glistening pink on that coldness—
for to lick your skin would be a sin
in public—
condemned for boldness.

Although it uses vivid imagery to describe a soda shop, the real purpose of this poem is to reveal something about the relationship between two people. Write a piece that uses a specific location as a way of introducing a larger theme.

"Ice-cream is exquisite. What a pity it isn't illegal." —Voltaire

Keywords: Sweet Tasty Melt Festival

winter's here

by Julie Brown

every year, it's always the same
the brown, rough statues stand tall
feet firmly planted in the ground
hoping to grow, reaching the sky
just out of grasp
then come the pesky green dots
spots of color—until mid-spring
then they are in full force
waving, swinging, attracting attention
the trees just sigh and stand
by autumn, they've had enough
they start to burn the leaves off
slowly, one by one
green to yellow to orange to red to
    brown
as they fall, the trees regret
winter's here and they've lost their coats

Do you have a favorite season? Using colorful imagery, describe that season and tell of several activities you like to take part in during that time of year.

"I like trees because they seem more resigned to the way they have to live than other things do." —Willa Cather

Keywords: Seasons   Nature   Leaves   Yellow

Smoldering Grass and Slithering Mice

by Martha Walker

Who can understand their dreams?
The dark man on the corner leans
Against the house under the stars
He hears the sound of dancing cars.

They jump and leap and spin around.
The quiet man lies on the ground.
In his hand he holds a stick
The man performs a magic trick.

The stars burst open in the sky
While nearby flies a butterfly,
And the grass goes up in the flames
The man sighs and his head hangs.

I watch him secretly from the cave
His body limp I try to save.
The stoplight hisses green and red
The noisy message hurts my head.

A hawk hops toward the ground.
The mouse slithers without a sound.
Moonbeams toward the corner fly
Around the bend and pierce my eye.

The dark man stands facing the door.
He's finished leading his final tour.
The people, worthless, stop and stand
And I hold a stick in my hand.

This poem opens with a question about dreams. Psychologists believe that dreams are indications of our subconscious thoughts. Discuss in detail one or more of the dreams you have had, and reveal what you think it means.

*"If I create from the heart, nearly everything works;
if from the head, almost nothing."* —Marc Chagall

Keywords: Darkness   Alone   Magic   Secret

Where I'm From

by Lisa Logsdon

I'm from lake effect,
From cotton candy bombardments
And blue crispy pathways.
I am from icicle trees,
Bending their branches to shake hands with the
    snow.
(shifting, shimmering silence is loud).

I am from three dogs, four cats, one horse and a
    chicken.
They all had their tricks when we had the right
    treats.

I am from the tire swing,
From cider-drenched air, cicada's tambourines,
And the hot sawdust perfume of grandpa's
    garage.
I am from clothesline windows and berry bush
    curtains,
From settle down and speak up,
And children are seen but not heard.
I'm from the clean plate club,
Where the amount of my love equals the
    amount that I eat.

I'm from Parkman, Burton and Troy,
From launching rocks at the sun like a fish out of
    water.
I'm from my father's greasy hands
That threw softballs with the fireflies.
I'm from my mother's good faith,
And achievements without payoff.
I'm from a one-armed coat hanger,
from unfinished business.
I'm a work in progress,
Painting on the canvas of my life.

This poem is written in free verse: that is, without a set pattern of meter or rhyme. Create a similar poem in which you use the first person to describe yourself and your origins. First do so with a strict rhyme scheme; then write it again, this time making sure *not* to rhyme. Which do you find is easier? Which sounds better?

*"Some people are your relatives but others are your ancestors, and you choose the ones you
want to have as ancestors. You create yourself out of those values."* —Ralph Ellison

Keywords: Ancestors   History   Self   Painting

Life Expectancy

by Cynthia Needle

Growing old.
Privilege or curse?
Consider the latter.
Some say it's much worse.

We've all heard the saying
From which truth is wrung:
Better to grow old
Than to die while you're young.

Youth and wonder.
Promise and pleasure.
Discoveries.
Dreams to be dreamt.
Eager to have all,
A life must be spent.

Some spend theirs wisely.
Some waste theirs away.
Some have them stolen too soon.

But oh! What a great ride,
This life that I've lived.

I've seen many places.
I've walked many miles.
That's why when I pass on,
I'll do so with smiles.

This poem begins with an implied question based on contrasting or differing ideas and ends with a declarative sentence. Develop a composition in which you ask a similar question related to any aspect of life. Discuss possible answers to your question before drawing your final conclusion.

"Life expectancy would grow by leaps and bounds if green vegetables smelled as good as bacon." —*Doug Larson*

Keywords: Aging   Life   Contentment   Satisfaction

Quiet Entities

by Mignon Self

When there are quiet times,
Thoughts in between crowded spaces in
    my mind,
I think of the entities that bind the time in
    packages
Wrapped with colored twine.

Bubbles, spheres of rainbows floating in
    the air.
Laughter, sounds from happy children
    playing.

Butterflies
drifting softly in the golden wind.
Violets, blooming vivid among the
    greenery, lie.

Kisses, a touch of love from deep within.
Glances, eyes that sparkle to say, "I'm here!"

Wine, the soothing taste that tickles as it goes
    down.
Clean sheets, crisp rough smells of speckled
    drops of sun.

Stars, shooting through the evening skies.
Hands that hold secrets of the brownie's past,

Sunlight drifting dots of dust giving life,
The entities of a crowded mind.

Bubbles, rainbows, butterflies, violets, and *drops of sun* are among the colorful images the poet uses to describe what goes on in her mind. Write a poem or prose composition in which you use as many colorful images as possible to describe your thoughts during quiet moments in your own life.

"Peace comes from within. Do not seek it without." –Siddhārtha Gautama Buddha

Keywords: Bubbles   Yesterday   Love   Solitude

The Absence of Color

by Cynthia Staples

Does sadness have a color?
Muted blue perhaps tinged with gray.
White with ash layered throughout like Morbier cheese?
Not black. Black is beautiful
As are gold, brown, and green.
They indicate life.
Sadness equals absence
Of light and color and warmth.
Arctic white then, yes,
That's the color of sadness.

This poem describes emotional states in terms of color.
Describe the feelings you experience when you see certain
colors. Try to come up with unconventional colors, such as
"arctic white" or "white with ash layered throughout like
Morbier cheese." What color descriptions can you think of?

"Sorrow breaks seasons and reposing hours,
Makes the night morning, and the noontide night."
—*Brakenbury, in* Richard III *by William Shakespeare*

Keywords: Black   White   Sadness   Cheese

Forever

by Brian Guido

A flower grew
In a corner of my garden.
Nearby, weeds waited
For it to wilt and die.
"Go away," whispered the flower.
"Soon *you* will die!
But I will live forever."

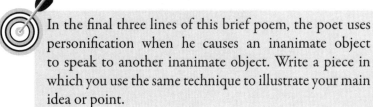

In the final three lines of this brief poem, the poet uses personification when he causes an inanimate object to speak to another inanimate object. Write a piece in which you use the same technique to illustrate your main idea or point.

"A morning-glory at my window satisfies me more than the metaphysics of books." —Walt Whitman

Keywords: Weeds   Metaphor   Petal   Garden

I Love a Parade

by Kristel Greenlove

Listen!

Can you hear it?
Can you see them come?

The tweedle-de-tweet of the
    piccolo.
The pounding of the drum.
The brilliant blare of the sounding
    brass.
The sudden shock of the cymbal
    clash.

The cadence of those marching
    feet.
Marching, marching.
Down the street.

Look!
There they are!

Here they come!

"The one thing I never want to see again is a military parade."   —*Ulysses S. Grant*

Keywords: Drums   Music   Uniforms   Spectators

Four Haiku

by Cynthia Lee Katona

Woman in burka
hands her license to a cop.
Does the picture match?

Generosity—
To give us a chance to give,
beggars work non-stop.

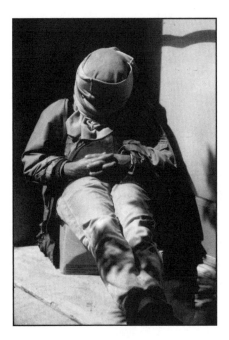

Bums mutter in streets
"OK baby, yeah, yeah, you bad."
The words keep them warm.

Human pincushions
Vie with mimes and fire eaters
For smiles and loose change.

Great Grandfather's Watch

by Betty Bowman

I still have great grandfather's watch.
It gleams in its golden case.
My mother kept it all her life
Displayed in a prominent place.

Just how he acquired it
Mother never did tell.
Not one of those memories was told
About long ago days
When she was a child
And her grandfather was old.

So now when I muse
Of those times Mother spent
With her old granddad,
I wonder:
Did she wheedle him
Into checking the time
And checking again and again?

The way children do,
You know.
"What time is it grandpa?" she'd ask
Just to see
The golden watch glow.

Then I wonder if
Great grandpa ever
Was late.
With a watch such as his
How could he miss
An important time or a date?

Perhaps my late husband—
Late even in life—
Had he worn such a watch
When alive,
Would not have been late,
As he so often was,
And perhaps he might still be alive!

"Either he's dead or my watch has stopped." —Groucho Marx

Keywords: Time   Grandpa   Memories   Gold

A Full Purple Crown

by Timothy San Pedro

For the first time in my life
I saw an artichoke bloom.
The heart, which we all crave,
Was pushed to the top
Toward the sun like
A hungry mouth to a bosom.
All around, the once supple
Leaves with fleshy meat
Were pushed outward as if humbly
Bowing to a crown.
A full purple crown
With jewels of bees and butterflies
And hummingbirds and water beads.

Too often, this plant's bloom is
Never to be seen,
Imprisoned
By immaturity, plucked before
Its true beauty is revealed
To the world.

Too often we
Are plucked from the planet
Before our true potential is
Squashed by money, greed,
Competition, and selfishness.
Will we ever have the chance
To bloom? To have jewels of
Caring, compassion, selflessness and trust?

When will our crowns show?

This poem uses metaphor to compare artichokes to people. What is the author trying to say? Do you think the metaphor is effective? Think about some metaphors you could use to provide insight into the theme of your next work.

"You are built not to shrink down to less, but to blossom into more." —*Oprah Winfrey*

Keywords:　　Self　　Maturity　　Growth　　Fulfillment

Letter to Urban Youth

by Timothy San Pedro

Don't apologize.
Run against the grain
Of a society that doesn't see you.
Yell through lips
Tightened by those who fought
Without knives or guns.
Allow one worn pencil to become
Unlimited ammunition.
No eraser.

Don't apologize
For telling your story
Of cement schoolyards,
Of barbed fences,
Of hoops with no nets,
Of schools with tattered books,
Of teachers with hardened hearts.

Don't apologize
For living
A life of poverty,
For richness isn't found in money,
But in love
For family,
For friends,
For people who see you as
Their inspiration, their future.

Don't apologize.
Run against the grain
Of a society that is forced to see you
Speak.

"He that respects himself is safe from others; he wears a coat of mail that none can pierce." —*Henry Wadsworth Longfellow*

Keywords: Respect   Education   Environment   Independence

For Jordan and Jackson
(With Love From Mom)

by Janet Vincent

"How many children do you have?"
I heard the voice say.
"I have a son who's nineteen.
He's my pride and joy."
But inside I'm shouting,
"I have *another* boy."

His name is Jackson
My son, who's in heaven,
I miss him so much.
In March he'd be seven.

But I answer intently
About the boy who is with me,
"My Jordan is my refuge
Of parenthood on earth.
I'm as proud as can be
Of this boy since his birth."

"I'm lucky to have them," I tell myself
    often,
And then I recall that tiny white coffin.

So, to answer your question,
I hope you will listen.
I have <u>two</u> sons:
One in my heart and one out and about.
They're both special to me.
Of that I've no doubt.

This poem is a lamentation over the loss of a loved one, as well as an affirmation of life. If you have experienced the loss of someone you love, use this poem as a guide to writing about your own loss. Make sure to include how this loss affected your perspective of life.

"Children are living jewels dropped unsustained from heaven." —Robert Pollok

Keywords: Children   Loss   Grieve   Deceased

Foreign Fish

by Laura Pastuszek

Two strangers from two different sands
Observe the gathering of food
In a foreign land

How beautiful and plentiful the sea must be
Remarks one to the other
The reply is not of glee

It is the raping of oceans
Taking more than necessary
A crime of epic proportions

A culture far removed
Lives to feed its own
Without an invitation for others to approve

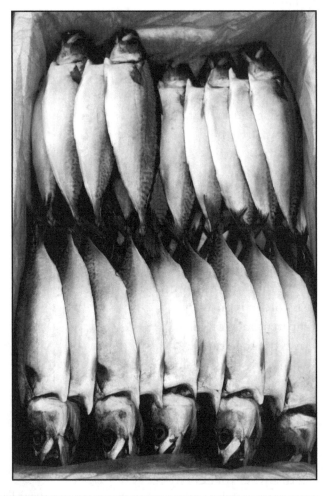

What do you think of this poem's message? Do you agree with the author's point of view? Think about some ways you think humankind misuses the environment. Choose one to write about, discuss the problem, and suggest a solution.

"Three quarters of the miseries and misunderstandings in the world would finish if people were to put on the shoes of their adversaries and understood their points of view." —*Mahatma Gandhi*

Keywords: Food   Sea   Fish   Excess

Going My Own Way

by Laura Pastuszek

Alone
in the midst of so many
I exist and I wonder
Enraptured by the magnificence
of
new discoveries
Dare I step across the norm
and welcome the intense waves of curiosity
Casting all caution aside
I walk where passion points
Obeying the intense quest within
I soar into uncharted heights of life

The author of this poem indicates the need to "soar into uncharted heights of life." What problems would you encounter if you chose to "step across the norm" and change your life in a dramatic way? How do you think your friends and family would respond to the change?

"The journey of a thousand miles begins with a single step." —Lao Tzu

Keywords: Life   Bird   Journey   Curiosity

A Salesman From Greer

by Betty Bowman

There once was a salesman from Greer
Who drove with his phone to his ear.
While he talked he was struck
By an oncoming truck
Thus ending his call and career.

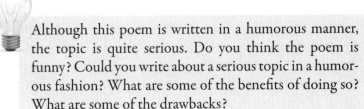

Although this poem is written in a humorous manner, the topic is quite serious. Do you think the poem is funny? Could you write about a serious topic in a humorous fashion? What are some of the benefits of doing so? What are some of the drawbacks?

"Fate is shaped half by expectation, half by inattention" —Rose, *in* The Joy Luck Club *by Amy Tan*

Keywords: Communication   Accident   Inattentiveness   Distraction

A Snapshot Look

by Kym Sheehan

Fragile spindles lay at rest after years of toil.
I miss the snapshot look of
left hand atop the right.
The yellowed, wrinkled mass became one.
Her hands were neatly trimmed,
but no manicure here.
Each scar and wrinkle represented
a day of hard work.
Her fragile hands rested upon the blue
   crocheted blanket
that shrouded her knees.
For the most part they lay motionless
A twitch here, a slight movement there
Those long slender fingers lost their
   strength long ago.
Gone too is the skin's elasticity
Like the blanket, the skin drapes across its subject.
Those brittle hands—oh so cold!
Cold hands—warm heart
Movement toward the teacup is viewed as slow motion.
The clinking cup against the saucer
highlights the lack of control.
Drops of tannic acid dot a trail from table to lap.
The cup shakes as if the earth were moving.
Another set of clinking sounds signals the end of activity.
The yellowed, wrinkled mass returns to stillness.

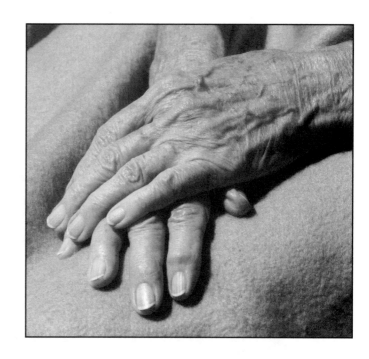

"It is autumn; not without
But within me is the cold.
Youth and spring are all about;
It is I that have grown old."
—*Henry Wadsworth Longfellow*

Keywords: Hands   Elderly   Reminisce   Wrinkles

Intimacy

by Kym Sheehan

Intimacy in black and white
A momentary peace
A cacophony of silence
Amid wet boots, fear, friend, and foe.
A façade
Stares that say I know
Stares of disbelief
Shoelace strings ties that bind
Intimacy in black and white.

"Intimacy" and its accompanying photograph present the concept of a close relationship between two people. Note how the imagery of boots and shoelaces is used—what effect does this produce? Think about some everyday objects that you can use to help illustrate a relationship with someone close to you.

*"I've noticed nearly all the dead
Were hardly more than boys."*
—Grantland Rice

Keywords: War   Soldier   Shoelace   Help

No Zac Efron

by Elizabeth Guy

He's no Zac Efron
I'm sure you'd agree,
But he's kind of cute I think.
With a slow easy smile
That's part of his style
And a little "come here" wink.

His tattoos cover much that's not
    seen
But at least there's no ring in his nose.
'Though his brain's not too keen,
If you know what I mean,
And he favors the oddest of clothes,
Yet, he's the one I chose.

I don't understand it myself.

So I guess it must be this:
'Though he belches and scratches
And snores
And sucks his teeth with a hiss,
I can never, ever resist
When he holds me and gives me a
    kiss!

"Anyone who's a great kisser I'm always interested in." —*Cher*

Keywords: Tattoo   Kiss   Attraction   Clothing

sunsparks
by Karen Topham

it's your hair that i notice first
streaked with morning
it frames your face
you lying there eyes closed
soft breath not quite there
unmoving
i follow its path as it bends the sheet
and i can touch you
touch what i feel is you

in the spark of daylight
you'll rise
pull on the wrinkled shirt from last night
say something you think is beautiful
drink some coffee
from behind my paper
and drive away
leaving a kiss on my lips
and a hole in my heart
where a fire ought to be

"If we do meet again, we'll smile indeed;
If not, 'tis true this parting was well made."
—*Cassius, in* Julius Caesar *by William Shakespeare*

Keywords: Daylight   Water   Sparkle   Disappointment

The Kiss I Got From You

by Christopher Thomas

There's a kiss that says I love you.
There's a kiss that says I care.
There's a kiss that proves our friendship.
There's a kiss that we can share.

There's a kiss that's not so honest,
And a kiss that's one too few.
But the kiss that I most treasure
Is the kiss I got from you.

Note how the second and fourth lines of each stanza of this poem rhyme: *care* and *share, few* and *you.* Write a poem that follows a similar rhyme scheme; then try writing a poem where the first and third lines rhyme instead. Which poem sounds better? Which do you prefer?

"Any man who can drive safely while kissing a pretty girl is simply not giving the kiss the attention it deserves." —Albert Einstein

Keywords: Smooch   Happy   Kiss   Treasure

The Last Day

by Lisa Logsdon

As I watch the sun rising
Over the fencerow glistening
On the muscled backs of horses,
I marvel at its relentless hunger
For travel between seasons.
The garden spider, laboring in his
    web
Tells me I'm clumsy by comparison
While I stumble closer
To hear him whisper my name.
I listen to the katydids,
And later, the crickets,
Wishing I had the courage
To raise my voice in unison
With so many others
Just once.
Barefoot, I wade in the cool, dusty
    earth,
Knowing even nonliving things
Like fire and ice
Have a pulse
And an influence.
The heat of the sun
Soaks deep as my bones.
I know this welcome joy
Has been there every day of my life,
If only I had chosen to—embrace it.
I lie in the warm, waving grass,
The setting sun gleaming gold on the green,
This is proof: Whitman was right

When he called them leaves.
As the moon rises,
I continue to lie in stillness
Amid the dronings of tree frogs
And winks of fireflies
In open conversation with the stars,
Waiting to fly.

"Keep your sense of proportion by regularly, preferably daily, visiting the natural world."   —*Caitlin Matthews*

Keywords: Seasons   Silhouette   Courage   Earth

Four Haiku

by Cynthia Lee Katona

Pandas in London.
Polar bears sweating in Rome.
What were they thinking?

The weather's too warm
The sphinx surprisingly small.
Might as well stay home.

Fish or fisherman.
A golden trout hits the lure.
Who is more surprised?

As everyone knows
The blackboard consumes the chalk.
Things at rest endure

Paper

by Gabrielle Lehmann

One day she met a charming man
Whose heart was made of paper
Beneath a latticed wooden cage
And skin as thin as vapor
With fingers wrapped in threads of red
And gold, no metal bands instead
Now taking hers in his he said
"My dear you scant could fathom
How laurels sit atop the head
Of one who's never had them."

"But follow me, my dear," said he
"I will bestow you treasure
And it will be, quite certainly,
Beyond all hope of measure"
The darling dear allowed him near
For through his pane of cellophane
So certain was she his veneer
And self could only be the same

An eon came and ages went
And though her love presented
A lavish wealth of great extent
His spouse was not contented

Beneath the strings his fingers bled
The plaster held no polish
No man beneath the ruby red
Which wind could not demolish
He held no secret in his breast
His ribcage rattled hollow
A heartless jest that proved at best
A tonic hard to swallow.

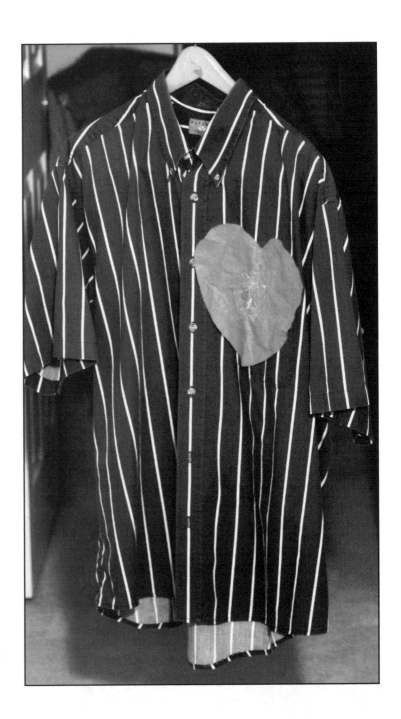

"Love is blind, marriage is the eye-opener."
—*Pauline Thomason*

Keywords: Veneer   Red   Disappointment   Secret

---

scream (after Munch)

by Karen Topham

what rawness then
what orange blue intensity
what whirling winding nightmare
infests your soul
when like a man possessed
you turn your back on
the sweetness of the day—
the harbor rich with spreading sails
the sunset rolling waves across the
    sky—
and staring into empty space
or at some demon gnawing at your
    mind
you lift your hands to your face
hold tightly to your melting
frameless form
and wait to hear
the heavens
when they scream

In this poem, the poet says that a negative attitude toward life is like a "demon gnawing at your mind," creating misery and unhappiness. Think of some instances in your life when you had a negative attitude, and try to think of some good metaphors to describe your behavior and emotion at the time.

"Anything, anything would be better than this agony of mind, this creeping pain that gnaws and fumbles and caresses one and never hurts quite enough." —Jean-Paul Sartre

Keywords: Nightmare   Space   Horror   Emotion

Jed
by Jeffrey Nichols

There once was a pirate named Jed
Who preferred that his peppers be red.
So he ate fifteen dozen
That he got from his cousin,
And now poor old Jed is quite dead.

One Hot Pepper
by Inez Airing

Some peppers are hot.
Some peppers are mild.
You're one hot pepper.
'Cause you drive me wild.

 Have you ever eaten food that was too spicy? If so, write about the food in detail, your reaction upon eating it, and the responses of any others who were with you at the time. Use sense impressions.

"I really was getting a bit bored with the piano. . . I just needed a new taste, kind of like another spice, so I got into the red pepper." —*Tori Amos*

KEYWORDS: Spice   Limerick   Pirate   Pepper

Advice

by Cynthia Needle

Listen up, girls!
Men don't understand women,
But it's not their fault.
It's just the rules of the game.
Remember, Martians and Venusians
Have decidedly different brains.

He doesn't get
Why she loves shopping,
Or why she wears
Those come hither clothes
And then says, "Don't you dare."

He just doesn't get all that makeup,
The lipstick, the liners, the hairspray,
The perfumes, the creams for her skin,
Ten different polishes for her nails,
A purse you could cram a car in.

Always changing her clothes
And changing her mind!
It makes a guy want to shout.
It just doesn't make sense to a man.
What's all the darn fuss about?

Nope, guys don't understand girls
With their fripperies, fidgets and frills.
They just don't get it.

But remember—
Likewise,
Girls don't seem to
Understand guys.

"American women expect to find in their husbands a perfection that English women only hope to find in their butlers." —W. Somerset Maugham

Keywords: Fripperies   Shopping   Provocative   Understanding

The Bridge

by Kym Sheehan

We named it The Singing Bridge.
Its small expanse connects and divides us.
Spanning the creek that leads to sleepy coastal
   towns,
It's been silver, gray, and green.
Peeling layers of paint are speckled with rust,
While starbursts of burnt sienna
Surround the rivets holding it together.

Oh, but it still sings!
When we drive across, its metal floor serenades us.
As we bounce, it hums louder and louder.
Then SMACK! We hit pavement.

Once across, a quick left and we park by the docks.
The odor of brackish water fills our nostrils.
We ignore the "Live Lobsters" sign and trudge
Down the bank
To the water's edge.

High tide with no boat traffic.
The surface water glistens;
But there's darkness below
As a breeze caresses the bridge,
While all the while it sings
And makes beautiful music.

"I stood on the bridge at midnight,
As the clocks were striking the hour"
—Henry Wadsworth Longfellow

Keywords: Music   Link   Odor   Darkness

Approaching Autumn

by Laura Lee

I love those sometimes mornings in late
    summer
When the air seems like an apple, tangy crisp
Cool, tasting sweetly on the tongue,
The white and yellow heat of summer fading
In the waning light of autumn's mellow sun.

Long since, fresh spring disappeared,
Its lovely blossoms browning at each edge.
Too soon, summer's fullness was upon us.
It drowsed and dreamed
In heated grass and sedge.

Now I await the fruited harvest.
As ripened colors burst upon my plate,
Sumptuous and succulent
Rich, redolent, and ripe.
I shall savor autumn's flavor bite by bite.

I shall feast upon life's autumn.
Devour each dimming, lazy day.
Treasure lengthened shadows in the twilight,
For my cold winter isn't far away.

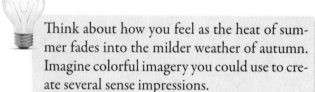

Think about how you feel as the heat of summer fades into the milder weather of autumn. Imagine colorful imagery you could use to create several sense impressions.

*"Delicious autumn! My very soul is wedded to it, and if I were a bird I would fly
about the earth seeking the successive autumns."* —*George Eliot*

Keywords: Apples   Taste   Harvest   Red

Sonnet 18

by William Shakespeare

Shall I compare thee to a summer's day?
Thou art more lovely and more temperate:
Rough winds do shake the darling buds of
   May,
And summer's lease hath all too short a date.
Sometime too hot the eye of heaven shines,
And often is his gold complexion dimm'd;
And every fair from fair sometime declines,
By chance, or nature's changing course
   untrimm'd;
But thy eternal summer shall not fade,
Nor lose possession of that fair thou ow'st;
Nor shall Death brag thou wander'st in his
   shade,
When in eternal lines to time thou grow'st:
   So long as men can breathe or eyes can see,
   So long lives this, and this gives life to thee.

Sonnet 18.5
(A Parody)

by Hank Kellner

Shall I compare thee to a clump of clay?
Thou art more gloomy and intemperate:
Rough winds do turn your hair to hay,
And winter's lease hath all too short a date.
Sometime through clouds the eye of heaven
   shines,
And always are his rays of light unglimm'd;
And every fair from fair oftimes declines,
By time, or many ruthless years untrimm'd;
So look not to your friends for timely aid,
Nor pray for help you surely need the most,
For Death will brag thou wand'rest in his shade,
When as they must your bones will turn to toast.
   So long as men can walk and tongues can wag,
   So long lives this, and this says you're a hag.

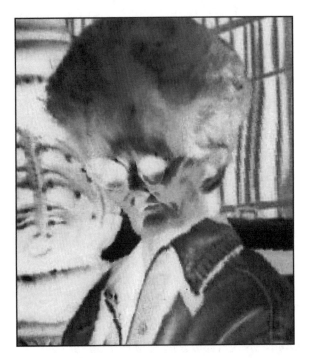

"Beauty is in the eye of the beholder." —*Margaret Wolfe Hungerford*

Keywords: Contrast   Beauty   Ugly   Personification

September Day

by Lila Mackey

It's a crystal bright
champagne September day.
The sky is crisp and blue.
I'm glad to be alive.
There's not a cloud in view.

I shake my head and wonder why
you'd want to turn away
from nature's wondrous pride
to sit inside, to slouch and hide,
on such a lovely day.

That's why I lift my voice to say,
"Get off that couch you lazy bum
so I won't have to shout
to make you understand at last
what real life's all about!"

 Between TV, computers, and video games, the temptation to stay indoors is greater than ever. Do you like to go outside? What do you think "real life's all about"? Write a piece that vents similar frustration at someone you know who spends too much time inside—or, if that person is you, write a piece in which you defend your point of view.

"Life goes by pretty fast. If you don't stop and look around once in a while,
you could miss it." —Ferris Bueller, in Ferris Bueller's Day Off

Keywords: Passive   Inert   Lazy   Couch

From the Love of My Parents

by Michele Kelley

I'm from my parents,
and their parents,
and all the parents before them.

From the frothy beer of Germany,
From the rotting russets of Ireland,
From calloused joints and pioneer dreams
In smoke-filled cabins of logs.

I'm from hog holler, cattle cuss, soil till men
who labored from dawn to dusk.
I'm from women who fried chicken, canned
    beans,
and hopped from the table to serve ice with
    tea.

I'm from women who served family first,
filled their plates last
and thought nothing of it.

I'm from people who wore hardwood pews
    smooth
With thanksgiving, praise, and plentiful sin.
From men well-respected.

And women well-loved.
From people who bore every wrinkle and
    frown
And always moved upward
Rather than down.

I'm from Lukes and Kings and Abels.
Murphys, Vawters, Bullucks, and Wrights.
From the love of my parents
From the long winter nights.

Many people enjoy gathering information about their ancestors. Either through the Internet or by interviewing a parent, grandparent, or great-grandparent, find out more about your ancestors. Write a composition in which you reveal your findings. Include as many family members as you can.

*"It is worthwhile for anyone to have behind him a few generations
of honest, hard-working ancestry."* —*John P. Marquand*

Keywords: Origins   Nationality   Parents   Workers

Boredom Is Rage Spread Thin

by Sarah Neil

The clock on the wall is a time bomb
I've been in this classroom for years

My stomach grumbles
My fingers wrap around my silken hair
The boy next to me smells of cologne
Girls pass notes when teacher's not looking
I reminisce of morning coffee on my tongue
My senses scream boredom
As I count the seconds to freedom
Tick-tock

The teacher tries to capture my attention
But the boy's cologne gives me a headache
Outside, the sun shines bright
Promising hope for afternoon pleasure
Tick-tock

Boredom is rage spread thin, I once read on a
    website

The monotone voice of educated machinery
    clogs my mind
The teacher dissects the Civil War before
Assigning lengthy homework
Again, sleepy Sarah refuses
To read 20 pages of tiny text crammed into
    wide pages
Tick-tock

The classroom door fades away as I realize that
Lunchtime won't come
In my near future
To free me from my classroom prison
Tick-tock-tick-tock-tick-tock

Think about a time in your life when you experienced extreme boredom. Where was it? What were you doing, or supposed to be doing? What would you have rather been doing? Did it make you angry?

"Boredom, after all, is a form of criticism." —*Wendell Phillips*

Keywords: Time   School   Boredom   Senses

Contentment

by Jakub Misztal

Sunlight peers through
hotel bedroom shutters
to find . . .
a rusted iron headboard,
dirty and neglected,
inside a sepia tinted world.

All is peaceful in the early stillness,
some people stirring,
others yet in slumber
by themselves
or with another.

Outside, a quiet murmur rises.
Somewhere a small dog yaps.
A man rests a moment on a bench
tired from his morning run.
Nearby a forest lush with green

Like the sun, we are all reluctant
to rise and start another day.
There is no greater peace, it seems
than in our beds
still warm from body heat
and dreams.

In the opening lines, this poet uses personification when talking about the sun (note the use of the word *peers*). In the closing stanza, the poet uses simile to compare the sun to people. Write a poem or essay in which you use either of these literary devices—or both—to humanize an inanimate object. What effect does this produce?

"The secret of contentment is knowing how to enjoy what you have,
and to be able to lose all desire for things beyond your reach." —Lin Yutang

Keywords: Peace   Solitude   Sunlight   Forest

Solitary Meaning

by Sheila Cooperman

Bare-cold worn floors
Worn by passersby that inhabit lonely places
Confined within walls that speak great
    sounds
Of lonely lives

Empty portraits on the wall
No commitment or warmth
Just there
Portraits with no more meaning than a
    pitcher or a washbasin
No more importance than bare brass hooks
As insignificant as a ragged towel
And threadbare shirts

Is the window open letting in newness?
Is the window closed imprisoning one
    comfortable in a barren world?
What is there is telling
What isn't there, even more

If what we have reflects importance
Then what is there
is barren
But perhaps, more important
is what is not seen
Perhaps the richness of that solitary life
Lives elsewhere
Something that cannot be reflected in the
    collection of things
Because things cannot do justice

*"Life is for each man a solitary
cell whose walls are mirrors."*
—Eugene O'Neill

Keywords: Barren   Missing   Rooms   Solitary

---

photos hidden away

by Karen Topham

i still can't look at the pictures.
so many years later,
the thick white ash
a fragment of a
bad dream,
the reams of papers
raining
from the smoky sky
in a nightmare hurricane
just an image from
some long past mirage,
and the headlines—
the headlines—
called up in the animated
dust
of no-longer buildings
and used-to-be people—
the headlines
i read then, and
folded away
carefully
to keep for
someone else's posterity and
never have seen again
and never will
bring the surreal
vision to the too real
world
where the pictures
of flames shooting from

buildings
of buildings collapsing
into smoke
are not magicians' illusions
as they should be
as they would be if
the world were
sane.

In this poem, the poet discusses her response to photographs of the attack on the World Trade Center in New York City on September 11, 2001. Consider one or more photographs that may have had a powerful effect on you, and describe in detail your response to those images.

"The camera can photograph thought." —Dirk Bogarde

Keywords: Vision   Impressions   Despair   Nightmare

No Dough to Buy Two Pickles

by David Henry

I want to travel far and wide
To places far away.
I want to travel now and hide
If only for a day.

But every time I plan to go,
I count my dimes and nickels,
And find to my despair my dough
Won't even buy two pickles.

That's why it's here at home I'll stay
While others get to go,
Until somehow I find a way
To rustle up more dough.

Many people feel that anticipating a journey is often more rewarding than arriving at a destination. Write about a time in your life when you looked forward to visiting a place only to be disappointed after you arrived. Be sure to tell what you expected to find as opposed to what you actually discovered.

"For my part, I travel not to go anywhere, but to go. I travel for travel's sake. The great affair is to move." —Robert Louis Stevenson

Keywords: Voyage   Yearning   Money   Pickles

Four Haiku

by Cynthia Needle

The clock's ticking hand
Counts life's seconds endlessly
Right up to the end.

First love is crystal
Many faceted and pure
Easily shattered.

Sun sparkles through leaves,
A burst of Autumn color
Winter lies in wait.

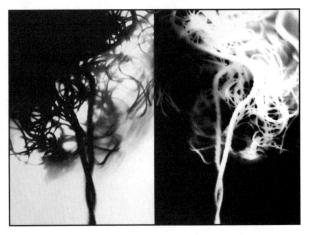

Twisted threads of lives
Unravel in confusion
A wild hopeless snarl.

A Grandmother's Heart

by Erick Moore

A grandmother's heart is a special
  place
You can read what it holds
by the smile on her face
Within her heart memories are
  dear
Memories of grandchildren
Laughter and cheer
Within her heart her grandchild
  will live
And her heart will not burst
For it holds people dear
Forever my Grandma
Forever my friend.

Grandmothers and grandfathers are important people in our lives. Write a description of a grandparent with whom you have had an especially close relationship. Include a physical description of your subject, and cite two or more ways in which that person has affected your life in a positive way.

*"Being pretty on the inside means you don't hit your brother and you eat all your peas—
that's what my grandma taught me."* —*Philip Dormer Stanhope (Lord Chesterfield)*

Keywords: Grandma   Heart   Memories   Peas

Beyond the Window

by Nichola Cody

I cannot see beyond the curtain
That cloaks my window.
But if I could, what would I see?
A field of wheat? A city street?
A cloudless sky? Cars rushing by?

I cannot see beyond the curtain
That cloaks my window
Unless I push aside the
flimsy cloth
And look beyond the glass.

Written in the first person, "Beyond the Window" poses a series of questions that remain unanswered because the author "cannot see beyond the curtain" that cloaks the window. What might you see if you could see beyond the curtain that cloaks *your* window? What would you hope to see? What wouldn't you?

"Better keep yourself clean and bright; you are the window through which you must see the world." —*George Bernard Shaw*

Keywords: Shadows   Light   Vision   Questions

Lily Loves the Lantern Man

by Rachael Penn

Lily loves the lantern man
who comes round town with his oilcan
and brings a box of broken wicks
with which to fix the candlesticks.

The other ladies tell her no
she must stay back or else she'll go.
Be forced to wander all the night
with only love and loss as light

but Lily loves his lovely eyes
they flicker, sickly fireflies
in a face that's gone to waste
from years of running, years of haste.
The ladies tell her, 'he brings death!
if he goes by you, hold your breath!'
and Lily knows the marsh is cruel
(would gladly steal a love-torn fool).

"O Leerie, I'll go round at night and light the lamps with you!"　　—Robert Louis Stevenson

Keywords:　　Lanterns　　Nighttime　　Candles　　Danger

Summer Storms

by Cynthia Staples

I miss summer storms,
Deafening noise, blinding light.
You know—the ones with rolling thunder,
Trailing white lightning in their wake,
Sheets of rain falling like milk from the sky.

We were trembling children.
As we peered past drawn curtains,
The storm seemed unending.

But then poof! Like magic it stopped,
Leaving silence in the air.
Darkness parted for the sun. Birds sang.

All that remained
Were puddles and leaves strewn across
The front porch. We stepped outside
Into a golden light as though
God had scrubbed the world clean
Just for us.

We played until sunset
And lightning bugs came out
To dance with the stars.

Recall a time in your life when you experienced a severe storm, tornado, or hurricane. Using as much imagery as possible, describe the event in terms of the physical setting, as well as in terms of your feelings during and after its occurrence.

"Birds sing after a storm; why shouldn't people feel as free to delight in whatever sunlight remains to them?" —*Rose Kennedy*

Keywords: Power   Lightning   Relief   Protracted

Eulogy for a Cat

by Kristel Greenlove

She was a curious
bundle of fur.
I named her Puff,
not for "the magic dragon,"
but for her pastel colors—
as though she'd been daubed
with a powder puff:
a dusty, saucy ball of fluff.
I thought she'd stay a few
short years
and die an early death
like so many cats
who die sometimes
before they've grown.
Surprise!
She didn't know she was a cat
and thus
due for an early demise,
and so she stayed
and played and napped
and sought out any spare
empty lap,
and roamed the house
on silent cat feet.
Through good and bad times she
    survived.
The years passed on.

Still, Puff retained that regal air
with which all cats are born.
Soon twenty years had passed
when on one sunny day
I found her small soft body there
curled in an old armchair.
I cried for hours on that day—
my cat Puff had slipped away.

Many people have experienced the loss of a beloved pet. If this has happened to you, write a composition in which you describe your pet in detail and your time together. Tell why your pet was special, and discuss the emotions you felt after your pet died. If you've never had a pet, write about what kind of pet you would like to have or, if you don't want one, explain why.

"The Naming of Cats is a difficult matter" —T. S. Eliot

Keywords: Feline   Pets   Memories   Dignity

Manhattan Reveries

by Jakub Misztal

The rain engulfs
Stark city streets
That gasp for air.

On a deserted street
Near a corner eatery,
A pretty girl stands
Smoking a cigarette.
I didn't know her name.
In contrast to the city's gray
And the brown of the diner,
The girl's glistening hair,
Against a neck white and marbled,
Recalls another girl I knew.

A taxi honks its horn,
The girl sighs,
The taxi pulls away.
Lights flicker.

At the subway station
Homeless people
Seek shelter in restrooms
And in rumbling trains
Where gunshots
Won't keep them up at night.

 This poem contrasts negative images of the city to positive images of a pretty girl to create a particular mood. Write a composition in which you contrast, or show the difference, between two people, places, or things. What kind of mood are you trying to create?

"City life—millions of people being lonesome together." —Henry David Thoreau

Keywords: Solitude Noise Rain Subway

Not Me!

by Brian Guido

You think I stole the cookies?
You think I climbed onto the
    counter,
Reached for the cookie jar,
And took it down?

You think I ate the cookies?
That one by one I broke them in
    half,
Chewed them up, and swallowed
    them
While no one was looking?

You don't believe me when I say,
"My sister stole the cookies
And ate them
And didn't even share with me"?

How could that be?
Why can't you see
It had to be my sister?
And not me!

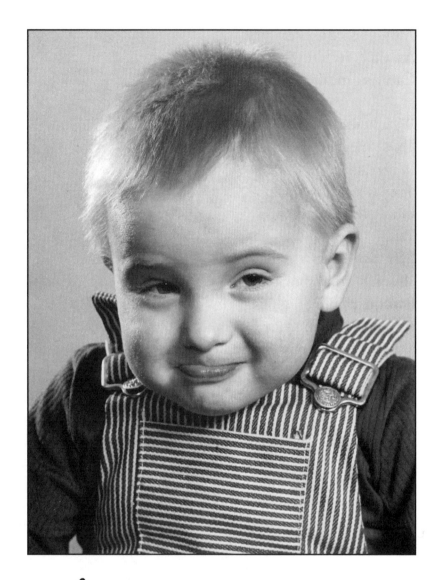

 Has one of your siblings ever accused you of something you didn't do? And has that person unjustly reported you to your parents? Write a composition in which you discuss the event. Tell what you were accused of, how your parents responded, and what the final outcome to the situation was.

"The three-year-old who lies about taking a cookie really isn't a liar after all. He simply can't control his impulses." —Cathy Rindner Tempelsman

Keywords: Guilt   Siblings   Truth   Innocence

Look Beyond the Ocean

by Christopher Thomas

Alone, I face the sea
As waves rush toward the shore
Carrying messages unheard.

What will they say,
Those silent thoughts,
When at last
They whisper to the sand
On which I stand?

"The world awaits," they cry.
"Look beyond the ocean,
Past the clouds
And out beyond the sky
Where you will find yourself."

 What does the author of this poem mean when he writes that you should look " . . . beyond the sky/Where you will find yourself?" Where should you look? Have you ever found answers to questions in unexpected ways?

"As for the future, your task is not to foresee it, but to enable it." —*Antoine de Saint-Exupéry*

Keywords: Ocean   Message   Meaning   Thoughts

A Bad Dream

by Faith Hooper

Night and day
Filled with fear, raging in the human mind.
Imagination spiraling out of control—
Is it true? Is it real?
Thoughts unspoken,
Gone unnoticed.
Releasing fury
Through your mind.
The Hole!

The Black hole!
The intense, never-ending black hole
Sending your thoughts racing.
Constant fear.
Every moment turned cold and dark.
Every thought gone bad.
Never to leave the hole.
Not ever.
Day or night.

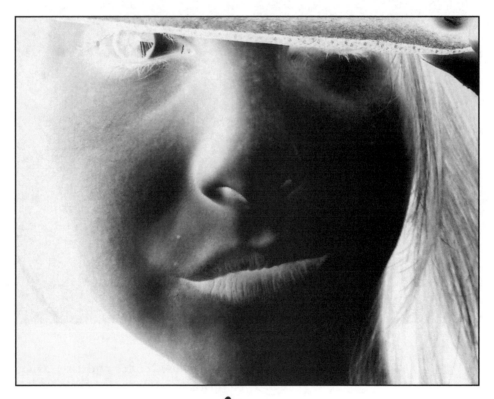

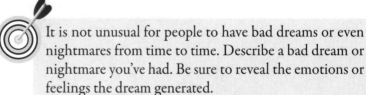

It is not unusual for people to have bad dreams or even nightmares from time to time. Describe a bad dream or nightmare you've had. Be sure to reveal the emotions or feelings the dream generated.

"Obviously one must hold oneself responsible for the evil impulses of one's dreams." —*Sigmund Freud*

Keywords: Negative   Anger   Eyes   Reality

Longing for the Riviera

by Anna Catherine

Coffee in the food court
amid plastic potted palms
fast food and flashing neon
in the air conditioned mall

lacks the carefree charm of

latte at an open air café
in the dappled shade of trees
on cobbled streets
lined with cottage shops.

There's really no comparison.

 This poet uses coffee and latte as entry points into a comparison between two environments. Think of some objects that you might use to define the environments in your life. Using this poem as a model, write a poem of your own in the same style as this one.

"No one can understand the truth until he drinks of coffee's frothy goodness." —*Sheik Abd-al-Kadir*

Keywords: Aroma   Desire   Location   Mall

Grandmother

by Mara Dukats

Your furrowed hands, spotted with
   the years,
your fingernails, so subtly earthen,
your slender, crooked fingers busy,
as we sit at the edge of the grove,
pitting harvested cherries with
   bobby pins.

Anchored on the stump, you're
   poised,
cradling between your knees the
   metal pot
into which drop, our sour cherries.

The pot fills unexpectedly (for me)
though you have always known
how simply one can fill the years
with marmalade.

Look at the quotation that accompanies this poem. Write a composition in which you explore the ways your grandparents play the roles of parents, teachers, and/or friends in your life. Cite as many specific examples as possible.

"A grandmother is a little bit parent, a little bit teacher, and a little bit best friend." —*Author Unknown*

Keywords: Memories   Cherries   Hands   Grove

In the Course of a Life

by Kristen Autumn Shortley

I hold no demons,
I hold no lies,
I keep that land of promise deep
   inside.
A basin of wrongs,
A cauldron of rights,
All in the course of a life.
Numerous regrets
On headstrong ears,
All hoping that that person would
   hear.
In the course of a life
Not all will lend that unwavering
   attention,
But I make the effort in hopes that
One day
You will listen.

In the body of this poem, the author alludes to problems she has had communicating with another person. In the last few lines of the poem, however, she expresses her hope that she will eventually be successful. Think about a situation in which you have unsuccessfully tried to communicate with someone. Did you give up? Are you still trying? Do you think you will one day succeed?

"You seldom listen to me, and when you do you don't hear, and when you do hear you hear wrong, and even when you hear right you change it so fast that it's never the same." —*Marjorie Kellogg*

Keywords: Relationships Understanding Regrets Attention

Memorial

by Lila Mackey

A lonely bagpipe wailed
One warm Memorial Day.

A small child placed
A white rose
On a monument of gray.

Proud veterans stood in stiff salute.
Winds caused the flags to snap.
While somewhere out of sight
A bugler sounded taps.

On every cheek a tear,
We stood in silence near a tree
And were reminded then and
    there
That freedom's never free.

 It's important to remember the hard work and sacrifice that members of the military dedicate to our country. If you have friends or relatives who have served or are currently serving, write letters to those people in which you express your appreciation for their service.

"The dead soldier's silence sings our national anthem."   —*Aaron Kilbourn*

Keywords: Memorial   Statue   Salute   Flag

To life, well-lived

by Mara Dukats

Summer's voice tips out into the
    wind and back
over the hundreds of roads we've
    traveled
to a Pentwater winter several
    moons beyond
the first buttercups that mark the
    edges of my road
and Deb, singing of old friends in
    denim.

Her blue gray eyes laugh with
    frayed threads and faded
    wrinkles
like stories, that unravel the depth
    of evening.
In the morning she rises, gathers
    summer in her
palms and sifts its moments like
    gold . . .

The roads in "To life, well-lived" are a metaphor: they symbolize the experiences the author has had with a friend over a long period of time. Using vivid imagery, reflect on the time you have spent with a friend or relative during your lifetime. Tell how the relationship has affected your life.

"Spend the afternoon. You can't take it with you." —*Annie Dillard*

Keywords: Denim   Buttercups   Wrinkles   Friends

Time

by Faith Hooper

It's the time for change
The time is here.
It's the time for new,
The time is here.
It's the time for love,
The time is here.
It's the time for patience,
The time is here.
It's the time for laughter,
The time is here.
It's the time for faith,
The time is here.
It's the time for life.
The time is now.

This poem consists of one long stanza in which the word "time" appears in every line. Why do you think the author chose to use such repetition? Do you think it's effective? Write a poem of your own in which you repeat a word, phrase, or sentence to emphasize the theme.

"The time is right to do what is right." —*Martin Luther King, Jr.*

Keywords: Calendar   Metronome   Change   Time

The Mathematics of Hate

by Timothy San Pedro

Hate,
When matched with more hate,
Does not cancel out.
It only doubles.

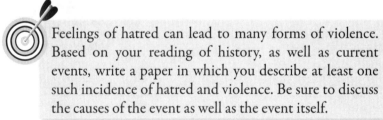

Feelings of hatred can lead to many forms of violence. Based on your reading of history, as well as current events, write a paper in which you describe at least one such incidence of hatred and violence. Be sure to discuss the causes of the event as well as the event itself.

"I will permit no man to narrow and degrade my soul by making me hate him." —*Booker T. Washington*

Keywords: Prejudice   Irrational   Intensify   Degrade

Fall Fever

by Amy Lyons

Leaves float undecidedly, my aches
    each colored in crimson and
    gold,
Strewn about streets and lawns, no
    longer hidden in the landscape
Their hues prick my senses alive
The sun's warmth quickens my
    pulse, pumping purple 'til it
    bursts to red.
I drive on, the picture outside
    now a blur of beauty and pain
    smeared in waxy oils
I turn up the music, each guitar
    chord plucks at untouched
    nerve endings,
Awakening that seasonal desire to
    be in love, be loved.
Dream fragments piece together to
    fill the vacancy

Last night, he belonged to me when my mind slept and heart awoke
It wasn't my longing but ours—at last, a mutual resignation
Today, the sky bleeds peaches, canaries and scarlets,
Shards of unconsciousness falling around me

"Now Autumn's fire burns slowly along the woods,
And day by day the dead leaves fall and melt."
—William Allingham

Keywords: Leaves   Autumn   Desire   Loss

The First Morning of the Night

by Rose Scherlis

I woke up,
But the sun never rose.
The sky stayed melancholy black
And hollow as a brittle shell.
This was the eye of a hurricane,
Of dangerous cold and the dark's
    madness,
And I dreamed of oceans freezing
    over
Of waves carved out of ice,
Ships frozen in place
Between glass shards of salty spray
Like so many deer caught in
Dark, distant headlights.
Morning never came.
I closed the curtains
Against the burning dark
Turned the switch,
As white as bone,
And the world
Froze
With me.

"Hold fast to dreams
For if dreams die
Life is a broken-winged bird
That cannot fly."
—Langston Hughes

Keywords: Towers   Frozen   Skies   Anonymous

Walls

by Betty Bowman

Who hasn't met stone walls
That block the way?

Or climbed walls,
In frustration,
Or
In boredom on summer vacation?

It's not easy to judge
Whether walls are bad
Or good.
It would depend on which side
One has stood.

Of course
Walls have more than one side:
More than two sides too.
There's this side and that
And a third side that's flat,
Or maybe rounded.

A wall might pen you in
Or keep you out.
Or it could simply be
A problem you must solve.

But never doubt:
When you find a wall
It always has another side.

This poem uses walls as symbols of obstructions or problems all of us encounter at one time or another. Write a poem or essay in which you discuss one or more of the "walls" you have encountered during your lifetime. Reveal whether or not you were able to climb these walls.

"Before I built a wall I'd ask to know
What I was walling in or walling out . . ."
—Robert Frost

Keywords: Texture   Climb   Solid   Safe

Depression

by Briana Birt

I can't remember who I was,
Because she's just too far away,
The bad times seem to go slow,
The good times never seem to grow,
I can't take a step in either direction,
It's too far from in-between,
So it's time to say goodbye to what I
    really mean,
And tell everyone that I'm all right.

I'm not happy but I should be,
The scars won't seem to fade away,
The bruises still black and blue,
I can't tell if my mind is playing tricks,
Or maybe it's pure insanity,
I can't pinpoint the exact moment it
    started,
I just remember feeling like I was in
    somebody else's body.

Who I used to be is no longer there,
I can't laugh without a slight pain in my
    heart,
I can't smile without shedding tears in my eyes,
Feelings of emotions are all mixed together,
Confusion or frustration? I can't decipher which is
    which,
Pride or plain-out cynical? I can't think straight.

Depression isn't easy,
All I know is that I can't be who I was before.
Yet depression isn't hard,
You finally get to be who you really are,

The thing that was eating you inside,
They'd love to see you fall,
But kill to see you die,
You are beautiful,
But you tell yourself a lie.

It's time to stop playing the game,
They know your secret now,
Just put on your game face,
Take a deep breath,
And try to smile one last time.

*"A man is never the same for long. He is continually changing. He seldom
remains the same even for half an hour."* —George Gurdjieff

Keywords: Costumes   Hiding   Pretense   Menacing

Four Haiku

by Laura Lee

Moonbeams on water
The echoing call of an owl
Magic in the night

The half moon rises.
A silver leaf on velvet,
Wistful as a dream

Mouthful of ice cream
Cool green grass beneath bare feet
Smiling summer days

A cauldron of fire
Sinks behind the purple hills
Daring stars to fall

The Surprise Answer

by Ms. Amanda Jones's class, Clay Elementary School, Clay, KY

Terrifying trouble,
Horrible hole,
Easy to fix,

Scary mother,
Using that door was a bad idea.
Really wish I had listened.
Patiently waiting
Ruined my day,
I am mad.
Springy spoiled surprise.
Everyone hide!

A hole will be hard to explain.
Never do it again
Someone's coming!
Where are you?
Everything is
Ruined!

"Never tell people how to do things. Tell them what to do and they will surprise you with their ingenuity." —*General George S. Patton*

Keywords: Surrealism   Intrigue   Emptiness   Mystery

A Dream

by David Henry

A dream slipped into my room
The other night while I slept.

"Who are you, dream?"
I asked softly.

"I am you," she said.
"I am who you are,
And who you were,
And who you want to be."

"Then stay with me,"
I whispered.
"For if it's true
That you are me,
Then surely I am you."

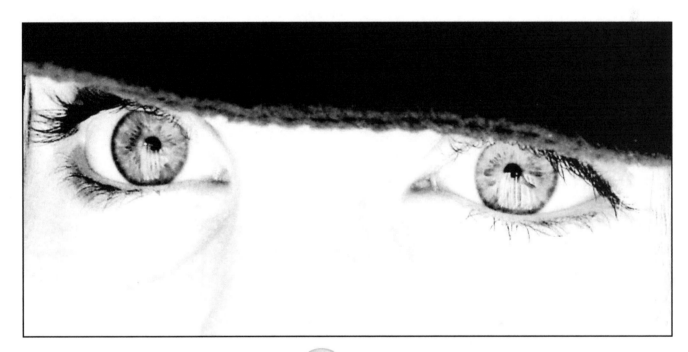

This poem describes a dream in which the dreamer meets another "self." Does this sound frightening to you? What would you ask yourself if you were to have such an experience? Would you want the dream to stay with you, or go away?

"All men dream: but not equally." —T. E. Lawrence (Lawrence of Arabia)

Keywords: Horror   Hypnotic   Self   Numb

I Am St. Joseph

by Stephanie Hartley

I am a busy Belt Highway,
holding the record for restaurants along my sides.
I am north, east, west and south end families.
I am bursting with college students nine months of the
    year.

I am quiet in the mornings.

Mustang games and flag football are family time here,
Swimsuits cling to sweaty bodies,
on their way to the pool,
When it's muggy and hot at 9 am.

People are friendly when they have to be,
but mostly slide by one another.
I am not scared by tornado warnings or blizzards
just losing cable.
I am not in a hurry to smooth my roads or curbs.

But I'll let you know if you need to mow. . .

My cinemas are always full;
what else will you do on a Friday night?
I am close to Kansas City,
so when you're running late for a flight;
In exploration of a foreign town,
you can certainly make up the time.

I encourage you to get out and see the world
Because I know I'll always be your home.

I am St. Joseph.

"Towered cities please us then,
And the busy hum of men."
—*John Milton*

Keywords: Crowded   Loud   Discover   Excitement

Alone on a Bench

by Hank Kellner

Why do you sit alone
On a bench in the city
While people rush past
Unseeing?
Are you tired, weary,
Thoughtful?
Or do you just prefer
To sit alone
On a bench
In the city
While people rush past
Unseeing?

In the first four lines of this poem the author asks a man why he sits on a bench alone in a busy city. Assume that you are the person sitting on the bench and in a short poem of your own, answer the questions in the first person.

"I don't want to be alone, I want to be left alone." —Audrey Hepburn

Keywords: Waiting   Boredom   Discouraged   Meditative

Bridge to Anywhere

by Elizabeth V. Best

I am a bridge that leads to here or there,
A pathway that extends to anywhere.
I shake with winds, but still I stand.
Should you lurch and fall,
Embrace uncertainty, for you can only slip
Between the creaking planks of your former
    self
And land on a new level with me.

Beyond the view of my highest truss,
Highways spawn, luring you away
Into detours and roundabouts
Unworn tracks lead you to the stillness of
    inner spaces;
Back to me through sun-mottled thistle and
    bracken.
Still, I stand absorbing ebb and flow:
Echoes from the much traveled roads.
I give passage to climbing aspirations and
    grounded realities.
I rise, buttressed and riveted yet flexible.

I feel passion swirl around my girders;
I hear needs and doubts and problems.
I witness memories dredged from
Hopes trapped, netted and choked
By too much think and see weed.
I extend myself above this undertow of daily
    hassle,
So tread water,
Reach out,
And you will touch me.

"All things and beings are a bridge to the Infinite." —*Adi Da Samraj*

Keywords: Connections   Rivers   Water   Vacation

The Old Guitarist

by William J. Small

Trembling twisted fingers
Sharpen against vibrating strings
He feels the noise misting his ears

A lone humble seagull
Struggling over the clouded waves
Sinking himself in an orchestra of
   emotion

Flailing, he can't escape
And he dresses himself with shame
That stands chiseled into his
   expression

Murky and cool he taps the
   echoing guitar
Crafting his voice through the
   strings
He flinches in regret

Teardrops mark his cheek
A humbling tribute to the past
He winces to forget

Misery drains his soul
As he pleads out
For echoless rest

Only to remember once again
That he is already dead

In "The Old Guitarist," the poet writes: "Teardrops mark his cheek/A humbling tribute to the past/He winces to forget." What do you think he is trying to forget? He "flinches in regret"—do you know what this feels like? Think about some regrets you have, and the kind of physical reaction you have when thinking about them.

"Lean your body forward slightly to support the guitar against your chest, for the poetry of the music should resound in your heart." —Andrés Segovia

| **Keywords:** | Lament | Rhythm | Strum | Regret |

Loneliness

by Elizabeth Guy

Loneliness is loud:
a white noise roar
a tinny taste that's swallowed
like a solid lump of air;
it turns the green soul brown and
 dry
with edges sere and crumbled;
it stretches thin and bare;
the taut threads tug.

and yet,
it seems to sit so loose,
a prison with an open door
through which one cannot pass.

This emptiness that fills one's every
 space—
to eat it, and yet live
and even laugh,
is one's greatest test of faith.

 Think about a time when you felt especially lonely. What happened to make you feel that way? What did you do? How were you able to overcome it?

"So lonely 'twas, that God himself
Scarce seemed there to be."
—Samuel Taylor Coleridge

Keywords: Lonely   Solitude   Boardwalk   Pensive

Above the Clouds

by Nichola Cody

If I could float
above the clouds,
unfettered,
free of shackles
that bind me
to the earth below,
what would I find?

Angels?
Lost friends?
A rainbow?
Lost love?
Truth?
Peace?

If I could float above the clouds,
Unfettered,
surely I would find
the answers.

But I can only float
in pools, in lakes,
or on the sea.
That's why I know
there's nothing
hidden in the clouds
for me to see.

"You must not blame me if I do talk to the clouds."   —Henry David Thoreau

Keywords: Flying   Clouds   Vastness   Daydreams

The Dog With No Name

by Rose Scherlis

Your furry head peeked out from under the table
So I dropped some fried plantain for you to
    enjoy.
You lived on a banana field in Costa Rica,
And it was beautiful, but the pesticides
For years underneath your delicate paws
Had twisted them until they grew like poison ivy
Bent in the wrong directions.
Your ear was tattered, a page in a book
With the corner folded down,
Signs of an ongoing war
With a world so menacing
When seen from way down there.
But still your tail wagged
Like a stick in the hand of a drummer,
And your fur shone
Mottled with brown splotches, just puddles of
    mud
Surrounding your two copper eyes.

Metaphors and similes are both methods of comparison. The difference between the two literary devices is that similes use the words "like" or "as" while metaphors do not. Look for examples of each in this poem. Then write a composition that uses at least one simile and one metaphor.

*"I think dogs are the most amazing creatures; they give unconditional love.
For me they are the role model for being alive."* —Gilda Radner

Keywords: Dogs   Loyalty   Friend   Dedication

Butterflies

by Cole Kim

Like butterflies
The years have passed
Too quickly, I'm afraid

I remember standing
In a field with you
While sunlight dressed the
    blossoms
In muted yellows
And kissed the butterflies . . .
Too soon gone.

But that was long ago
When first you held me close
And whispered words
That danced in the wind
And quickly disappeared.

So now I stand and wait
Hoping for butterflies to return
Although I know they won't.

Butterflies are fragile and fleeting. What else can you describe this way? Think of animals, objects, relationships, events, or even people. Choose one that has special meaning to you and write about it.

"The paired butterflies are already yellow with August
Over the grass in the West garden;
They hurt me. I grow older."
—Li Po, as translated by Ezra Pound

Keywords: Nature   Colors   Brevity   Fragility

A Happy Chair

by Elizabeth Guy

Behold, a happy chair.
Were I to rest on it,
Surely warmth would fill me.

Surely all my cares
Would disappear
Dissolve into the smile
That seeped right through me.

I could be a little child
Again
If only for a little while

And then,
Restored, renewed, refreshed
I'd continue on.

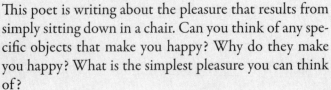

This poet is writing about the pleasure that results from simply sitting down in a chair. Can you think of any specific objects that make you happy? Why do they make you happy? What is the simplest pleasure you can think of?

"A table, a chair, a bowl of fruit and a violin: what else does a man need to be happy?" —*Albert Einstein*

Keywords: Smile   Sunshine   Whimsy   Respite

Doors of Persuasion

by Laura Pastuszek

How often life and the journey
Are intentional decisions carefully made.
The path is clear; the door is open.
The eager soul sets forth
On the road to purpose
Only to be exposed to more external
   choices:
Various interesting niches beckon,
Distracting the traveler
But perhaps eliciting new possibilities.

This poem speaks of doors we open with our own decisions and paths we may choose to follow. Describe a door of opportunity you have opened during your lifetime, and tell how doing so affected your life. Can you think of any metaphors besides "doors" to describe such an experience?

"The doors we open and close each day decide the lives we live." —Flora Whittemore

Keywords: Entrance   Doorway   Invitation   Possibility

Four Haiku

by Elizabeth Guy

Green leaves drip with dew
A brown bird flits from a tree
Sing! Long winter's done

Chaos in the streets
A boy stands at the window
Waiting for his dream

Bright artwork on brick
I want to live in pictures
It's easier there

Orange wedges tumble
A promise of succulence
Makes my mouth water.

Wish

by Brett Pepowski

little girl spies the door open free
short hair slaps neck as she skips down steps
trips and scrapes hand on gravel, no worries
(she keeps band-aids in her pocket for that sort of
    thing)
she's up and running in no time

today it's to the stream to dangle toe-tips in water
and the sky is so full of sun the light drips down
through trees onto leaves with a sparkling splash
she can practically feel it
sunlight taps small feet as they swing

it's off, it's off, it's off to the fields
her dog has been digging somewhere in the corn stalks
muddy paw prints bloom on her blouse
as he jumps up wagging to greet her

up to the pond her uncle dug
still a muddy hole, but he keeps dreaming
it's a pond, it's a pond, and she believes him
her parents won't let her swim
who knows what parasites are there young lady
so she hid her swimsuit in a tree and comes on days like this

band-aids and corn stalks, dog, pond, stream and woods
these are her summers, the suntan still shows
back in school every year boys flick paper wads and call her a sissy
but she can beat the fastest boy in a race
and she knows it

"In summer, the song sings itself." —*William Carlos Williams*

Keywords: Water   Summertime   Doors   Sparkle

Reflections on a Winter Painting

by Elizabeth Guy

I saw a winter painting and I smiled.
Then once again my brother lived.
Tall and strong, he pulled the sled
When I was just a little child.

Trees black laced against
An orange smear of sunset.
The evening star a diamond in the dusk.

Below, the crunch of snow beneath the runners.
Toes numb in buckled boots.
Frozen misted breath, and mittens caked with
    ice.
Riding like a small princess across a frozen
    tundra.

Home at last!
Stomping, laughing, pulling off our coats,
Breathing in the kitchen's fragrant warmth.
Fingers tingling underneath the tap.

Winter memories of my brother.
Rest in peace my childhood knight,
And angels guard your soul.

Now the rising pearl of moon
Casts its ghostly pale
Upon my withered lawn.
Frost lies everywhere—
Like fairy dust turned cold.

*"Winter, a lingering season, is a time to gather golden moments, embark upon
a sentimental journey, and enjoy every idle hour."* —*John Boswell*

Keywords: Sledding   Winter   Cold   Exhilarating

Faceless Man

by Cole Kim

Faceless you are
In your hat and coat.
Yet, faceless you are not
As you look upward,
A microphone held before you.

Of what do you sing,
Faceless man with face?

Of birds and bees and puffy clouds?
Of happiness that knows no bounds?
Of moments treasured as you float through life
Untouched by hardship, pain, and strife?

Or do you tell of dreams that rent
The night with fear and shame,
With memories so sad
You wish you could forget them?

Of what do you sing,
Faceless man with face?

Tell your story to the world,
And in that way
Reject the darkness of the sable night
That you may then
Stand proudly in the wonder of the light.

Contrast can be used in writing to illustrate different or opposing ideas. Here the poet uses a dramatic contrast in his description of a "faceless man with face." What do you think this line means? What kind of images come to mind? How does it relate to the rest of the poem?

"Learn from yesterday, live for today, hope for tomorrow." —*Albert Einstein*

Keywords: Drama   Regret   Agonize   Hidden

Four Haiku

by Elizabeth Guy

Life can box me in
Like a girl kept in a frame
Still I shop for shoes.

Peace lilies still bloom
In a world gone mad with war
Don't they realize?

Twisted strands of rope
Like so many lives entwined
Bonded together.

Bright and fragile blooms
Dazzle me with brilliance
Delicate as glass.

Self-Identification in the Crinkling of Fall

by William J. Small

The light glazes the treetops
A crisp crinkling ripple in my ear
I splash in the wind,
I grasp for the aftertaste of the moment,
Left behind by the blink of my eye

Like a mossy rock it slips through my mind
Deeper and deeper away

In a crescendo it once again erupts
As I feel the light shivering of the grass,
Against my restful body

I spin along with the Earth
As it tells me all its secrets
Of love, loss, and etc.

The only sounds trickle from a sparrow
Scatter from a squirrel
Tickle from a falling leaf
To create a stream of sounds

Oh Fall!
Bring change and beauty, as I grow old!
And now as I bathe in the angst of coming maturity
I pray to resemble the subtle whispery kisses of you.

Examine the way the poet has described familiar sights and sounds to evoke a brilliant autumn day, and note the reverie they inspire in him. Write a poem or other composition in which you describe a time, a place, or an experience that speaks to you in a similar way. Use as much vivid imagery as possible.

"Every leaf speaks bliss to me,
Fluttering from the autumn tree."
—*Emily Brontë*

Keywords: Leaves   Autumn   Endings   Bittersweet

Rainy Day Reverie

by Anna Catherine

rain runs in rivulets down the pane
blurring the world beyond
through the window mottled light
dances swirling through the glass
shifting shadows dance
shadows moving, melting
one into the other
ever changing memories
rain-washed dreams
long gone
dreaming all that was
dreaming all that might have been

 Write a piece about rain. Use imagery to evoke the feeling of a rainy day. Describe the sounds and the activities one might pursue. Would you rather run in the rain or remain snug and dry somewhere? Tell how you would feel in either situation.

"A rainy day is the perfect time for a walk in the woods." —Rachel Carson

Keywords: Window Rain Refuge Renewal

rainbow's end

by Karen Topham

rainbows do end
though scientists say
no, impossible
against the laws of nature

i know
i have seen
i have been there

driving through canada
past cloud-peaked mountains
on a winding highway
the burst of sky-color following us
painting the clouds
its palette the universe itself

we rolled along unthinking,
until around the bend we saw it:
the end
the spectrum stripes falling to the ground
right before our eyes
in the road just ahead

in future days
when dreams have blended with
the road dust
and tremors deep within
shake my foundation
under hazy gray skies

i long to recapture the moment of passing
when the lazy arcs of color stayed
before us until we drove right through them
and watched as, perhaps bewildered
they melted, diffused,
and disappeared into the canadian sky

*"The true harvest of my life is somewhat as intangible and indescribable as the tints of morning or evening.
It is a little star-dust caught, a segment of the rainbow which I have clutched."* —*Henry David Thoreau*

Keywords: Promise   Delight   Rainbows   Wonder

Skateboarding

by Rose Scherlis

Sometimes I glide, soar, weave
Duck under heavy, mournful
　　branches
Decorated in fragile autumn leaves
Like so many brilliant orange
　　faeries
Until I reach my destination:
An abandoned bridge to read
　　under,
A coffee shop or candy shop,
Or just an empty lot to carve
　　across
Sometimes I skate
As fast as I possibly can
Until the world blurs into a
　　colorful blend
Of distractions, possibilities, ideas.
Until day turns to night,
Sunsets sparkle across the horizon
　　like
Vivid necklaces of pink and red.
Until I lose track of time,
Lose track of myself.
Sometimes I skate.

Colorful images swirl and converge in this poem about the joy of skateboarding. Notice how the world blurs, and how the skater's mind becomes receptive to new ideas. Write a piece that describes one of your own favorite activities, and tell about the kinds of things you think about when you're doing it.

"These sports are just—you go do it, and you're doing it on your own. You don't have to answer to anyone." —Tony Hawk

Keywords:　　Motion　　Action　　Confusion　　Forgetting

Through the Looking Glass

by Nichola Cody

As I look back
through the lens of my life
I see I've been

Daughter,
Sister,
or Wife,

Aunt,
Niece,
and Mother—

Defined by others
and by my place
in their lives.

But now I wonder
what I will see
as I look to the future
with me as just me.

What would you see if you looked at your own life through a mirror or looking glass? A son or daughter? A student? A good friend? What defines you? What do you think others would see? How do you think your life will look 10, 15, or 20 years from now? How will the image in the mirror change?

"Vision is the art of seeing what is invisible to others." —Jonathan Swift

Keywords: Looking   Spying   Intruding   Curious

Where Is My Heart?

by Christiana Pontier

She left without question.
She left without reason.
She left without a care.
She left without remembering
to give me back my heart.
The part I let her have.
Where is my heart?

I went to her,
but she didn't have it.
She used it.
Then threw it away.
I've checked all the trash in my life.
I cannot find it.
Where is my heart?

I've seen her a few times.
She acts like she never had it:
like she never possessed my heart.
She acts like she didn't shatter it.
There is no remorse within her.
She doesn't care about my heart.
Where is my heart?

I will see her again very soon.
She will be waiting.
I know that she will be.
I will not be waiting for her.
She used my heart.
Now I cannot find it.
Where is my heart?

This poet uses short, stilted sentences with heavy repetition. What effect does this have? How could she have written this poem differently? Do you think it would be as effective?

"You flew off with the wings of my heart and left me flightless." —Stelle Atwater

Keywords: Pleading   Reaching   Despair   Hands

To Book Snobs Everywhere

by Lisa Blair

Reading can be personal;
Not everything has to be cerebral.

You prefer books of high culture,
Texts like renaissance sculpture.

My tastes are more prosaic;
I enjoy the formulaic.

I don't want to have to think
When I'd much rather slink

Off into my corner
And dive into dreams with no borders.

Vampires, fairies, blood and gore,
Monsters, romance, foreign shores.

Murder, mystery, magic, mayhem;
Maybe they're not *your* crème de la crème.

Your trash is my treasure;
Your disdain is my pleasure.

But you don't have to like my choices;
You don't have to hear my voices.

You read books of your choosing,
But you won't find me schmoozing

With some high-fallutin' text in my hand
To act like you up there on your grand stand.

I'll make my own reading adventure
Without concern about your censure.

Here's the thing about reading.
If we do it, we're both succeeding.

Look at the style and structure of this poem. Its defiant tone and rhyming couplets work to defend the author's reading preferences while dismissing the loftier preferences of others. Think about how you can express tone through the rhythm and rhyme of your words. Then try to write a poem in response to this one, taking the book snob's point of view.

"Always read something that will make you look good if you die in the middle of it." —P. J. O'Rourke

Keywords: Afternoons Books Quiet Adventure

Hope

by Laura Pastuszek

Hope grows
Even in the dearth
Of
Obvious
Nourishment

"Once you choose hope, anything's possible." —*Christopher Reeve*

Keywords: Possibilities   Beginnings   Tenacity   Overcoming

untitled

by Julie Brown

the page sits open like a great divide
inviting, begging the poet to begin
writing a masterpiece
sure to please the masses
but these things don't just materialize
a poem is not a car
you cannot turn the key and start
poems need inspiration
thought
hesitantly, thoughtfully the poet
raises a pen

as the pen tip nears the paper
quivering
the smooth white surface
and the rounded black tip
swirl into a magical unison
the words flow endlessly
effortlessly
the poet writes for days
the connection between
pen and paper is strong
until at last the poem is live

 This poet describes the process of writing a poem. Compare it with the quote by Robert Frost. Do you think writing poetry is difficult? How do you feel about using difficult or painful emotions as inspiration? Which do you find is easier: writing poetry from hardship or from joy?

"A poem . . . begins as a lump in the throat, a sense of wrong, a homesickness, a lovesickness." —Robert Frost

Keywords: Paper   Ink   Writing   Letters

The Pumpkin Sonnet
(With Apologies to Shakespeare)

by Cole Kim

Some say that cherries are the best to eat,
And some prefer potatoes that are fried,
But I think cherries are by far too sweet,
And fried potatoes I just can't abide.

Then there are those who claim zucchini's best
And those who like tomatoes as a treat.
But I don't think zucchinis pass the test
And 'maters aren't the best I think to eat.

Still others do prefer a plate of peas
Or plantains fried and salted to their taste.
But peas my palate surely do not please
And plantains I discard with timely haste.

So, pumpkins are the ones that catch my eye
Because I like to eat them in a pie.

This playful poem tackles a whimsical subject in the rigid, formal structure of a Shakespearean sonnet. Consider the rules of writing a sonnet: It requires 14 lines of 10 syllables each and a set rhyme scheme. Now try writing a sonnet of your own, on a subject of your choice.

"I would rather sit on a pumpkin and have it all to myself than be crowded on a velvet cushion." —Henry David Thoreau

Keywords: Orange   Harvest   October   Jack-o'-lanterns

Memory Quilt

by Lila Mackey

A blue chambray piece from
her late husband's shirt,
an old apron's calico scrap,
bright flowered strips
from a granddaughter's dress,
gathered, pieced in her lap.

Sunk there, ensconced
in the old battered chair,
specs atop the gray head,
eyes straining
to see tiny stitches
held near,
gnarled fingers
pull taut the fine thread.

Patching a patchwork,
making it whole,
tending,
mending
the tear in her soul.

This poem, about an old woman sewing a quilt, describes specific pieces of fabric, each with a life memory attached to it. Describe in detail some object in your own home that evokes specific memories and what those memories are. Is this an object that you cherish or one that you would prefer not to see?

"Our lives are like quilts—bits and pieces, joy and sorrow, stitched with love." —*Author Unknown*

Keywords: Quilts Remnants Frugality Memories

All Cooped Up

by Jake Kutchins

Like last week, and the week
　　before last
All I can feel is skin hugging my
　　fragile bones.

My dirty feathers bind me,
　　although I cannot fly
There is never a soul to be seen,
　　none but I.

Trapped, trapped alone in my
　　dusty cage
Night after night
I wish someone could come by
And teach me how to fly.

Oh, how it always is the same,
　　always, the same
Nothing around to share my pain.

Oh, how I wish I could fly.

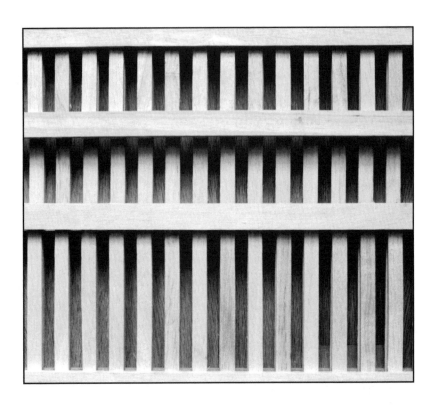

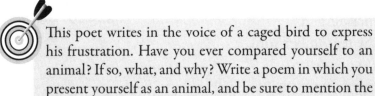 This poet writes in the voice of a caged bird to express his frustration. Have you ever compared yourself to an animal? If so, what, and why? Write a poem in which you present yourself as an animal, and be sure to mention the specific ways that you are similar.

"You can cage the singer but not the song." —*Harry Belafonte*

Keywords:　　Flying　　Caged　　Pain　　Fragile

© Prufrock Press Inc. • *Reflect and Write*

Permission is granted to photocopy or reproduce this page for single classroom use only.

110

Fabric

by Jakub Misztal

Consider it possible:
The slipping away of light
as a blanket of darkness
Surrounds all
As the blood,
Slows its descent to the heart.
And in one
Glorious moment the fabric of
    time parts
To reveal the mortal body.

Slowly the spirit crawls out,
And fades into the very same fabric
Sensing no danger but simply
    release and surrender
To a dim glow that recalls a
    memory
That was fond,
A grip that touched the heart,
A time where all was at its center and its place.
Nothing amiss.
Nothing wrong,
A warm feeling,

Until finally
The deepest most calming silence,
That this world has ever heard.

"Silence, beautiful voice!"   —*Alfred, Lord Tennyson*

Keywords: Moonlight   Eternity   Silence   Magic

Two Kids on Red Brick Canvas

by Cole Kim

Red brick forms the canvas
On which I see
A smiling man, a woman, and
A younger man whose head is lost
Behind the shadow of
A vent on which a cat rests,
Prepared to pounce . . .
Or so it seems.

Below and to the right,
A bearded man in black hat;
A musician in red hat;
And two children
Complete the scene.

Intrigued, I stop and say,
"Who are you?" to the smiling man.
He says nothing,
As do the woman, the bearded man,
And the red-hatted saxophone player.

The cat just purrs and looks at me
As if to ask, "Don't you know, you fool?"

The man without a head, of course, can't
    speak.

The children look at me
And smile as children do,
Then say, together,
 "We are those you see
And do not see.
We are you.
We are humanity."

Puzzled, I walk away
And think about the words
I heard from two kids painted
On red brick canvas.

*"I paint people, not because of what they are like, not exactly in spite of what they are like,
but how they happen to be."* —*Lucian Freud*

Keywords: Graffiti   Streets   Artists   Messages

Going Green

by Cynthia Needle

"Green" is the latest buzzword.
So politically right, you know,
Or maybe it's left, but nevertheless
Greener is where we must go.

Oh, not the green of envy
And not the green of greed
And not the green of
"Ohh! I shouldn't have eaten
    that!"
But the green that makes things
    grow.

Green energy—less fossil fuel.
Go green—recycle your waste.
Green grooming,
Green living,
Green cooking as well.
Green's the new sign of good taste.
Green has taken the country by
    storm
Green everything no doubt will
    soon be the norm.

But somehow I get it,
So here's what I'll do:
I'll eat only green foods,
And drive a green car.
I'll wear a green jacket
Green stockings and shoes,
If only you'll show me
Green cows in a zoo.

This poem expresses the writer's feelings about the current trend toward the conservation of our planet's resources. Compose a piece that describes in detail a trend, social convention, or behavior that is of interest to you. Be sure to cite specific examples to support your ideas.

"We do not inherit the earth from our ancestors, we borrow it from our children." —*Native American proverb*

Keywords: Growth   Freshness   Nature   Ecology

grief
by Inez Airing

emerging from the gray
grief-stricken gloom
the raucous fuchsia red
of one lone bloom
proclaims its victory over death
shouts *look*
and don't despair
life awaits you
everywhere

petals soft and sweet
unfold
hold the heart
in rapture
hypnotized
like some eternal life
now realized

The poem "grief" uses vivid imagery, symbolism, and personification to underscore its message. Note how the one flower blooming embodies the message and invites a positive response to a negative situation. Write a poem or other composition in which an inanimate object becomes the vehicle through which you express a major thought.

"In all things it is better to hope than to despair."   —*Johann Wolfgang von Goethe*

Keywords: Blossoming   Unfolding   Revealing   Fragrances

Gossip

by Lila Mackey

"There's a new man in town . . ."
the red hat gals babbled—
singles, and widows, and such.

They murmured and oh'd
at each episode
of the troubles he'd caused:
it was much!

And I must admit
it was hard to sit
and listen to all their dithering,
without giving in
to my own little sin
of subtle sarcasm, withering.

But over their heads
my witty remarks
flew with un-understood regard.
So, I guess I'll sit here
in my own little chair
and just listen—but oh my, it's hard!

Everyone hears gossip. Do you like to pass it on? Keep it to yourself? Ignore it? How do people sound when they're gossiping? Try to capture the sound and effect of gossip in a poem of your own.

"If you haven't got anything nice to say about anybody, come sit next to me." —*Alice Roosevelt Longworth*

Keywords: Moody   Isolated   Gossip   Sarcasm

Still the Bells

by Christiana Pontier

Why do your bells ring?
Why do they ringle and jingle?
Jingle and jangle?
Why do they ring?
Is there no hand to stop them?
Is there not a hand,
escorted by the sun's valiant rays,
reaching out to still them?
To stop them.
To stop them altogether.
To stop them forever.
To be stilled,
forever?

"Still the Bells" begins with a question, asks several more questions, and concludes with a final question. Can you answer them? What do you think the bells represent? Why do you suppose the poet is so concerned with them? What is the meaning of this poem?

"Never send to know for whom the bell tolls; it tolls for thee." —John Donne

Keywords: Bells   Alarm   Sunlight   Disturbance

Bees

by Judith Norberg

Ouch! That bee sting hurt!
I was three when
I let out a screech that rattled the
    trees
And deafened a few thousand bees.

From then on if bees came,
I'd go screaming away
Across the grass.
I was lucky I didn't fall on my
Head
And bump it,
Or scrape my knees.

I was really afraid of bees!

Even though they make honey.

So, thanks to the bees
For honey from flowers
In blossoming gardens
In wake of spring showers.

Even so,
When the bees come to visit,
I still scream with fright.
As I quickly take flight.
But that's not unusual.
Is it?

This poet describes a common reaction to bees. What frightens you? Think about one of your own frightening experiences, and consider whether or not you have been able to overcome your fear.

"When you go in search of honey, you must expect to be stung by bees." —*Joseph Joubert*

Keywords: Insect   Fear   Gardens   Pollination

Windmills

by Judith Norberg

I remember the barn,
Its door half open,
Its siding weathered and bleached
Like wood left too long
In sun and rain.

That's where we kept our pony.
Don Quixote was its name.

"We'll call him that," said grandpa,
"'Cause he was in a famous book."
And then he smiled and told me
About windmills.

"There's plenty of windmills
Still around," he said.
"They come in many sizes, colors,
And shapes."
He lit his pipe, smiled, and added,
"Look out for them."

I didn't understand what grandpa meant
Years ago when he stood near the barn
And talked of windmills.

But now I do,
For I have seen more than a score
Of windmills spinning through my mind
Like dust storms in a desert.
And when I did, I thought of grandpa
When he said, "Look out for them."

And so I have.

In the novel *Don Quixote,* the main character believes windmills to be giants and perceives them as threats. Have you ever imagined something to be a threat or problem, only to find out later that it was no big deal? How did you deal with these threats? What happened?

*"And the world is like an apple
Whirling silently in space,
Like the circles that you find
In the windmills of your mind."*
—from "The Windmills of Your Mind," by Alan and Marilyn Bergman and Michel Legrand

Keywords: Barns   Caution   Yesterdays   Advice

Continuity

by Laura Pastuszek

I am full of life
as my presence fills the air with
    sweetness.
Others delight in my beauty
and I am grateful for the
branches that undergird me.
For without them
I would not be
A place of refuge
For others to know
and feel welcomed to
create new life
placing an imprint of the process
on my safe and supple petals.

In this poem, the flower speaks as if it were human. The poet identifies with the flower and uses its qualities to express appreciation for her place in the world around her. Think of something in nature that you might compare yourself to. How are you similar? Write a poem using personification, in the style of this one.

"The continuity of life is never broken; the river flows onward and is lost to our sight" —*John Greenleaf Whittier*

Keywords: Refuge   Life   Nature   Reproduction

The Conductor

by Michele Kelley

When I hold the untouchable,
When I heed the dynamic unseen,
When I glimpse the marrow of a soul
And taste its fire upon my skin.

When the scent of the sum of many is one
Yet more than the singular whole,
In that moment of mystery
This servant of music knows All.

This poem tells of the deep connection and sense of awe that the speaker feels when conducting. Do you participate in any activities that make you feel this way? Write about something you do that provides you with great pleasure. This could be singing in a chorus, writing for the school paper, acting in a play, or any other activity. Include specific details that reveal why you enjoy this activity.

"It's the Power of the Almighty, the Splendor of Nature, and then you." —Al Franken

Keywords: Orchestra   Symphony   Leader   Coordinate

© Prufrock Press Inc. • *Reflect and Write*

120   Permission is granted to photocopy or reproduce this page for single classroom use only.

Waiting

by Brian Guido

I waited for a place to sit.
I waited for a train.
I waited for a good long bit.
I waited for a plane.

I waited for a waiter, too
I waited 'til my lips turned blue.
But 'though you say you love me
true,
I'll never, ever wait for you!

Waiting is something we have all experienced. When have you found yourself waiting, and how did you respond? Did you get impatient and bored, or were you excited? Do you ever enjoy waiting?

"Somewhere, something incredible is waiting to be known." —Carl Sagan

Keywords: Arches Travel Cultures Waiting

Take a Break

by Anna Catherine

Stop
What you're doing.
Take a break.
Sit down and rest.

Full steam ahead can be a
    mistake
Until you've thought it all
    through
And you know
What to do
And that it's for the best.

This is a test.

 What does this poem say to you? To what extent do you think before you act? Are these words good advice, or do you find this message too restrictive or patronizing? Explain why you feel the way you do.

"Live this day as if it were your last." —*Wayne Dyer*

Keywords: Handprint   Sign   Lifeline   Forbidden

Sculptor

by Amy Lyons

It began with a crack—
An exquisite pain awakened at the crevice
Then the gentlest chiseling with a focused
    deliberation
Gave way to undetectable beads of water from
    its overexposure
As he continued relentlessly to shape and
    repair
Until the muse, too, envisioned herself
    beyond her formless block
With delicate patience, his persistent hands,
    warm with an artist's passion
Melted away edges to smoothness
Until she took on a shape he knew was his
    masterpiece—
A sculpture that stood firm for both to admire

In "Sculptor," the poet describes the process required to create a statue out of stone. Write a poem in which you describe a process step by step. Your composition could be about anything you choose to write about. For example, you could describe how to make something, how to study, how to listen to music, or even how to brush your teeth. Be creative!

"I express myself in sculpture since I am not a poet." —Aristide Maillol

Keywords: Granite   Form   Sculpture   Passion

A New World Is Here

by Faith Hooper

A new world.
Starting fresh.
New hopes, new dreams.
Like a kid with a new gift.
Not knowing what to do with it.
Having a hard time exploring.
Trying to figure it all out,
All the new and wonderful things.
So many still left undiscovered.
Hoping the feeling stays.
Hoping it never fades away.
Hoping the niche is found.
Feeling like it belongs.
Wait is over.
Change is here.
Hope is found.
He is near.
Love is close.
A new world is here.

"Rarely have Americans lived through so much change, in so many ways, in so short a time."
—President William Jefferson "Bill" Clinton

Keywords: Change   Beginnings   Rebuilding   Promises

© Prufrock Press Inc. • *Reflect and Write*

124   Permission is granted to photocopy or reproduce this page for single classroom use only.

Outside My Window

by Mary Meyer

Barren branches bright with ice
sparkle in the winter light.

A red cardinal and his rosy mate
perch among the boughs.

A speckle-breasted flicker
With his nape of red, and
a black and white woodpecker
who sports a ruby head:
both are pecking for their prey.

A nuthatch scampers head first
down the tree,
a tiny feathered dart of
black and gray.

There, a brown and yellow flutter
of the golden finches waiting
to take their turns at the thistle feeder,
where a crowd is now abating.

A gray white-bellied junco scurries on the snow;
snatching scattered seed, he hops away
as a flash of blue and black scolds at his back—
the raucous, harsh complaining of a jay.
This bird-painted tree
is as lovely in the snow
as the Christmas tree that stood inside there
only a month ago.

"'Hear! hear!' screamed the jay from a neighboring tree, where I had heard a tittering for some time, 'winter has a concentrated and nutty kernel, if you know where to look for it.'" —*Henry David Thoreau*

Keywords: Tree   Season   Shelter   Wildlife

A New Generation

by Bambi Fischer

This is the hand that joined
      another.
It touches the shoulder of a
      hardworking man.
Together they tilled the land.
The lace of the dress,
The handsome suit,
The flowers,
The bowtie,
The elegant hat
Certainly represent a day of
      celebration.
The hands that joined each other
Are now one.
Husband and Wife
The beginning of a new generation
In America.

 This poem reads like a description of an old photograph, evoking the depicted couple, their relationship, and how they may have felt at the time this photo was taken. Choose an old family photo from your home and use it to write a similar piece. Don't worry if you don't know all the details behind it—use your imagination to make up your own!

"Newlyweds become oldyweds, and oldyweds are the reasons that families work."   —*Author Unknown*

Keywords: Ancestors   Eras   Photograph   Marriage

Dirty Asphalt

by Vic Capaul

Coasting on slippery tar
Carefully driving my car
Now we're entering a construction zone
Pay attention and don't get T-boned
This old road is getting wild
The suspense is not mild
Take the clear path out
Or you'll get stuck going round and about

The speed limit is getting higher
This car is becoming a flyer
The road under me gets cleaner
My attitude gets leaner
Ripping the rubber is now a tradition
The speedometer shows me my inhibitions
Old remission
New ambition

Describe your response to this poem. What does it seem to say about caution? About inhibition? Do you think this poem portrays a positive message? Why or why not?

"The best car safety device is a rear-view mirror with a cop in it." —Dudley Moore

Keywords:	Driving	Traffic	Signs	Speeding

A Forever's Goodbye

by William J. Small

Have you ever felt the lie?
That sparkle in the eye

A distant torch
As we approach your porch

The breeze!
The chiming trees!

Our eyes shut tight
In the forever dark night

A moment
A fragile threadless second
Burns the rhyme away

But only for one blissful jolt!
Oh the eternal joy!

You brush against my heart
Shifting we fall apart

You moved away
And now only our tree
   bark hearts remain

This poet uses a series of images to suggest a relationship between two people, culminating with the final line: "And now only our tree bark hearts remain." Think about a meaningful relationship you've had with someone, be it a family member, a friend, or a boyfriend or girlfriend. Are there any images you can use to illustrate your relationship?

"Promise me you'll never forget me because if I thought you would I'd never leave."
—*Christopher Robin, in* The House at Pooh Corner *by A. A. Milne*

Keywords: Separation   Farewell   Romance   Conclusion

Bill

by Elizabeth Guy

Bigger than me,
he was five, I was three.
He'd take my toys and run
and think it was fun.
I didn't agree.

We were ten and eight when
he taught me how to roller skate,
then teased me when I fell—splat!
Sprawled flat on the ground.
After that I skated when he wasn't around.

That summer at the lake
when we were twelve and ten,
he swam well then
while I seemed to take all day
to reach the floating raft not far away.

One day I floundered past my depth
when at my back I felt a forceful hand.
It pushed me, gasping,
to the shore where I could stand.
As I looked back.
he flashed a grin
as if to say,
Come on back in.

He was my hero then
as he is now.

He was my brother.
But he's gone,
and there won't be another.

This poem describes a sibling relationship and how it grew and changed through the years. Write about your own relationship with a brother, sister, or friend. Give specific examples of how you relate to one another. Include settings and events, and describe how you felt at those times.

"Teenagers too often have to deal with loss and death . . . how can young people deal with such tragedies?" —Andrew Shue

Keywords: Summer Childhood Siblings Death

The Greatest Generation

by Lisa Logsdon

My grandmother,
she wore her damage well—
The alcoholic husband, the womanizing father
The depression, and the war
Quietly raged against the cacophony of periwinkles
On her starched white shirt.
It hung from her in layers, from her apron to her skin,
But she stood impervious in her unbroken optimism.

"Your grandfather volunteered to cook
On the ship that brought him back from the war,"
She cackled. "The Brits were terrible cooks."
Fortunately for him,
Grams was territorial in her modest house.
Even the blitzkrieg wouldn't have made it in
Without first taking off its shoes.

In the kitchen,
the gathering place for family women,
I watch the sturdy forms of my great aunt and her
        sister
Performing enchantments through tendrils of steam,
Aimed at the rattling pots.
I think about the mettle that forged their generation,
Not the steel magnolias of the South,
But something stronger, quieter, fiercer.

Even their names were inflexible and rare.
Alone with my thoughts, I wonder.
When the dust settles on the last Irene, Loretta and
        Grace,
Who will hold us up?
Where is the greatness of my generation?
And if we were forced to rise, like them,
Would it be powerful and uncompromising,
Or would we point fingers and skulk away?

"A woman is like a teabag. You cannot tell how strong she is until you put her in hot water."   —*Nancy Reagan*

Keywords: Heritage   Family   Tradition   Stories

Taunting Voices

by Hillary Lockhart

No one understood the girl until
    they read the letter left behind.
It explained how she squeezed
    between lockers avoiding the
    bullies' surprising slaps, strong
bruising fists with forceful hits,
    hidden kicks,
followed with gleeful haunting
    laughter
and abusive chatter
with ugly, abstract disapproving
    frowns.

All her hope was released and lost
when she believed the taunting
    voices proclaiming
her unworthiness to live.
If only someone intervened, or
protested against the bullies'
    unfairness,
would she be today walking alongside
    of us, joking and daydreaming of a
    hopeful future?
If only someone was unafraid to share
    her hurt and pain, she prayed.
If only someone reached out . . .
If only someone cared . . .
If only . . .
If only . . .

This poem deals with the bullying of a young girl and its tragic outcome. Write a composition in which you describe a similar situation you have heard about, read about, or witnessed firsthand. Describe how it affected you. Discuss several ways by which you think such behavior could be controlled or eliminated.

"Never be bullied into silence. Never allow yourself to be made a victim. Accept no one's definition of your life, but define yourself." —Harvey Fierstein

Keywords: Bully   Advise   Intervene   Help

Shattered

by Sheila Cooperman

No right to feel so shattered
Before a window pane
Looking in
Broken webs of tangled strands
Connected in a maze of confusion
A beating heart
Like fluttering wings
Echoing through an empty shell
Suspended in midair
Beating and moving
Dead and stagnant

Put aside the web of the past
Tuck it away under a wing
Bury it
How hard to bury the crucial and
    the necessary
No right to feel so shattered

Yet
The breath catches in my throat
Tears sting my eyes
A lead filled weight
Dark invisible hands
Pressing me down

Get Off!

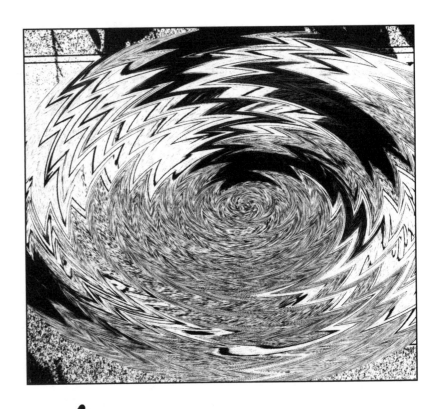

The author of this poem uses vivid imagery to illustrate negative attitudes or behaviors that have plagued her. In her conclusion she indicates that, although she has attempted to do so, she has been unable to "Put aside the web of the past." Create a composition in which you describe one or more aspects of yourself that you have tried unsuccessfully to change.

"Our joys as winged dreams do fly;
Why then should sorrow last?
Since grief but aggravates thy loss,
Grieve not for what is past."
—Thomas Percy

Keywords: Glass   Disappointment   Hope   Anger

Don't Go

by Sheila Cooperman

The sun winked as it turned to leave
Trailing behind, its colorful train.
"Don't leave," I implored, "It's far too soon.
　　The azure above still breathes."
But the solemn sun paid no heed to my
　　desperate pleas.
"Soon," it sighed. "Soon, I will return in
　　blazing glory.
Strong and defiant against the stranger's
　　fingers of bony cold.
Soon I will return to those that long
To be embraced by the soft heat of my love"

But now it was I who could not hear the
　　empty promise
"Don't leave," I begged. "It's far too soon.
For tomorrow's eyes may not gaze upon the
　　blue carpet of today's heaven.
Please listen. Tomorrow's eyes may only gaze
　　upon the gray that will reign supreme.
Don't go. It's far too soon.
Tomorrow may only see the colorless palette
　　of an empty heart
Don't go,"

But the sun began to fade
Its jaunty bounce slowed
As it began its sad and somber waltz
Without me.
"Don't leave," I demanded. "It's far too soon."

But the sun did not look back
Its colorful train following like an obedient
　　dog
"Goodnight," it whispered
"Don't leave," I screamed
But my lost companions in the sky
Took no heed of my lonely
Desperate pleas.

*"Don't leave me alone!
A cry in the night,
Of anguish heart-striking
Of soul-killing fright"
—Menolly, in* Dragonsinger *by Anne McCaffrey*

Keywords:　　Anguish　　Dependency　　Unhearing　　Desertion

Lone Ranger

by Diane Wahto

The masked rider
armed with the silver bullet of knowledge,
astride the white steed of pedantry,
clad in the black suit of mystery,
boldly confronts
the arrogant ignorance
of English majors
lined up in straight rows
of desks, ready
for the showdown
of mind against mind.

Never slipping, the mask speaks
disembodied truths,
nods, says ummm
to answers
that shoot out with
blind courage,
missing the mark,
but wounding
nonetheless.

The masked wonder-
teacher founders, wishes
he could reveal truth,
knowing he must always
be the one to say,
"But look at it this way,"
or "Don't you think . . . ?"

And sometimes one *will* see
and fly straight to the salient
point with unerring accuracy.

Who is the "Lone Ranger" of this poem?
What does he wish to do? Why doesn't
he? Do you think he should?

"It's easy to make a buck. It's a lot tougher to make a difference." —Tom Brokaw

Keywords: Learning Knowledge Questioning Truth

Fun House Reflection

by Matthew Bernbaum

I see me through their two-way mirror,
Twisted and distorted, misshapen
   and warped.
I see ugly and I see disgust,
I see horror and I see mistrust.
I see me through my one-way
   mirror,
Plain and flat, simple and clearer.
I see what they see: I see me.

But what do they see?
They see me through their two-
   way mirror,
Plain and flat, simple and clearer.
They see worried and they see
   confused,
They see hurt and they see used.

One by one their mirrors shatter.
They leave me confused, and soon
   I'm sadder.
My mirror now alone,
Reflects thoughts my own.
But what does it show me?
What would you see?
What is me?

In the first stanza of this poem the author uses mirrors to reveal his impressions of self. In the second stanza he asks what others see. In the final stanza, the mirrors shatter, and the poet asks the question: "What is me?" Write a poem or essay in which you describe yourself, both physically and emotionally, from someone else's point of view. How does it differ from your own?

"Life is a mirror and will reflect back to the thinker what he thinks into it." —Ernest Holmes

Keywords: Mirror   Distort   Confuse   Impression

Inspiration

by Becky Brown

So cheerful
Yet so grim
The inspiration hits
And the pencil caresses the paper
Turning dreams to realities

The words flow freely
Unhindered by the conscious
    mind
Simply written as thought
As fragments, piecing themselves
    together
From disorganization to art

The pencil writes still
As if it has a mind of its own
The words just keep coming
And you sit, helpless to stem the
    flow
Like the mouse versus the
    mountain

You keep your head down
So oblivious to the world
Until the poem is done
And the inspiration trickles away
Like the stream in the desert

When you write, do you find the "words flow freely" until "the inspiration trickles away"? Do you often find yourself inspired to write? How does it feel when you do? How does it feel when you don't? Think of imagery and metaphors to describe these sensations.

"You simply sit down at the typewriter, open your veins, and bleed." —Walter Wellesley "Red" Smith

Keywords: Writing   Poetry   Create   Author

Moon Sleep

by Sheila Cooperman

I put the moon to sleep tonight
It looked so drowsy
Its gray silvery tint fading
    imperceptibly
Slipping down into the dark
    blanket of sky
Sleep
I gave the moon permission
To close its weary eyes
To bathe in the misty glow of its
    silent night companions
Twinkling stars that melt the soft
    black sky

Eternal lights protecting,
    watching, accepting
"Sleep," I told the moon, "You are
    assured a place in my heart
Your shining glow shared with me when you are full and bold
Your soft shower when you are a shy sliver in the sky."

A small, slight smile
Just a reminder
I smile back, no reminder necessary
For when there is light, acceptance, protection
There is love

"Sleep," I told the moon
The night diamonds and I will
Protect your slumber.

"When twilight drops her curtain down
And pins it with a star
Remember that you have a friend
Though she may wander far."
—*Julia Bell, in* Anne of Green
Gables *by Lucy Maud Montgomery*

Keywords: Sleep   Dream   Protection   Permission

The Lone Wolf

by Becky Brown

See the lone wolf
Howling, silently
Howling over life, over loss
Over love, and the reality of life

He is howling, silently
As he looks to the clouds
Wondering how, what and why
And sinking, to his own state of
    mind

Watch him, and listen
To his most haunting howl
Screaming, "hear me"
But all the doubts still remain

He looks to the sky
A black mess of light
The distant stars shining
Like the lost rays of hope

His life, his loss, his love and his world
All converge into one;
A single, small entity
With the power to live, and to love

"Every wolf's and lion's howl
Raises from Hell a human soul."
    —*William Blake*

Keywords: Loss   Mourn   Animals   Desert

The Wrecking Yard

by Gabrielle Lehmann

The wrecking yard is full tonight, but it won't be for
    long
The wrecking yard is full for now—tomorrow, we'll
    be gone
We're all the things you never knew
You missed—the things you threw away
We're all abandoned, old and blue
Our life ends here because of you

The wrecking yard is full tonight
Of old machines and busted parts
The wrecking yard is full of stories—
Tales spun deep in hard-drive hearts
Each toy left here was once a friend
But now it seems we're all but lost
And what it comes to, in the end
Is when the time came, we were tossed
They're hard facts, here, to try and face
That we aren't all just here, misplaced
Maybe now we've been replaced,
Or maybe we were never really there for
    them at all
Or maybe now we're all a pile of bones,
    however small

And now it seems we're all forgotten—
All that's left is broken dreams
And we weren't broken, we aren't rotten
When we got here, we were clean
It seems somehow we've lost our purpose
Somehow we're now obsolete
Once all priceless, now we're worthless
Things have changed—we can't compete

Tonight the wrecking yard is full of click-track hearts
    and old machines
Tonight the wrecking yard is full—the wrecking yard
    is full of screams—
The crusher runs on overtime from evening on 'til
    dawn
To clear out our assembled line—
Tomorrow we'll be gone

The author of this poem uses a wrecking yard as a metaphor to present a dark perspective. Note how she uses imagery to create this effect. Write a poem or essay in which you use positive imagery to present a different view of life. Where does your piece take place? Make sure to include specific imagery and details.

"I only feel angry when I see waste. When I see people throwing away things we could use." —*Mother Teresa*

Keywords: Waste   Recycle   Discard   Unwanted

Dragonfly, Shelling

by Clara Quinlan

How silver clings to the light the rain

Stammering, its threaded wings
under the wind *see we all hold on*

with our many arms iridescent
body curled against the boat's pier,

magenta sheen, flecks of blue,
tiniest instance of

something I might walk toward
were I lost, were this world to carry me
no longer.

Its shell with shape with eyes
like it could be, again, in this stirring—

Collection *soft* of scraping leaves

soon dripping, a sound
you can count and in the numbering

the shore lit with the born
silver bodies from the pier
into the lapping and the one

in your hand, extended, transmuting the light.

Notice how the poet uses specific descriptors to evoke the shimmering image of the dragonfly, including colors and motion. Describe some familiar animal (perhaps a pet) using sense impressions to create a word portrait of your subject.

"Deep in the sun-searched growths the dragon-fly
Hangs like a blue thread loosened from the sky:—"
—*Dante Gabriel Rossetti*

Keywords: Delicate   Flotsam   Seashore   Iridescence

Winter Shore

by Clara Quinlan

Where the only sound
is the moan of the dark deep lake
you find me.
Against its own skins of
ice, the water's small equation of despair,
where fists of shore birds
exact themselves
into lines along the driftwood, shadows
stretching back to the undressed trees

How the heart looks back—boldly,
is undone—spare nothing of your arms to me.

And the rose of the sky
the white dog bulleting the birds
into a spattering of
wings, the waves, lit pink
slight fluttering of voice moving
through the ranks of quilted black things,
all the evening light descending—

our bodies
measuring years, mapping veins—

laced in silver in reflection
on this first shore:

where the world
returns us, one to the other,
the birds unflinching above

and this wind, I welcomed
through me, knew your hands before
they touched.

"A lake carries you into recesses of feeling otherwise impenetrable." —*William Wordsworth*

Keywords: Heart   Water   Recall   Love

In the Wild

by Erick Moore

In the wild I see
A great blue sky
Hanging over me
With clouds as white as snow
At night I see a soft glow.

In the wild I see
Cute little birds singing to me.
What beautiful songs they sing
With glee.

In the wild I see
A fawn and its mother
Dancing with gentle grace.

In the wild I see
Nature.

This poem attempts to convey the writer's sense of delight and discovery in nature. He writes of the "blue sky hanging" and the deer "dancing with gentle grace." Write a piece about your own response to being "in the wild," and use lively verbs and colorful images to reveal your feelings.

"The poetry of the earth is never dead." —*John Keats*

Keywords: Wilderness   Forests   Deer   Skies

The Blue Door

by Cynthia Needle

Right there
In the middle of the city
High above the alleyway
A blue door

A balcony haven
Bedecked in flowers
Beckoning the sun
A promise of warmth
Serenity

Behind that blue doorway
A cool and calm retreat
What secret pleasure
Lingers there inside
Above the street

Behind
A multi-paned
Azure stained
Unexpected door

 In this poem, the author writes about her response to seeing something unexpected. Wondering about it, she describes it in detail, including such contrasting sensory images as "A promise of warmth" and "A cool and calm retreat." Compose a similar poem about a place you have encountered in your own environment. Incorporate contrast and sensory images into your description.

"Blue color is everlastingly appointed by the Deity to be a source of delight." —*John Ruskin*

Keywords: Unexpected Mystery Serenity Secret

Chip Off the Old Block

by Mara Dukats

I needed to learn how to sink more
    putts
So you took me to the green.
Relax and enjoy yourself quietly,
    you said,
Golf, like poetry,
comes from the core—
the way you relate to the world in
    silence.

Gaze leisurely at the pattern of the
    grass blades,
Become familiar with their
Sharp shadows, their
shagginess
Golf, like poetry,
Needs a mind aware.

Freefall
Slow and smooth and steady
Be the tempo
Of a lazy day,
a baby elephant
Swinging its trunk
Ever so lightly
Through savannah grass.

Read the green
Watch balls bounce, roll.
Downslope, gravity,
All chip in.
Before you know it,
You're in the chips—
A poem in your pocket
Like a hole in one.

Think of an activity you particularly enjoy. Tell what it feels like to participate in the activity, and reveal what it means to you. Is there any way your activity can be used as a simile or metaphor?

"Golf is a spiritual game. It's like Zen. You have to let your mind take over."   —*Amy Alcott*

Keywords: Poetry   Green   Play   Writing

Yellow Bird

by Caroline Kerr

I wonder if she still cries when she hears
the somber voice of Cat Stevens
crackling wearily through the car radio
the way she did 10 years ago
as we drove through Birmingham, Alabama,
the hungry sunshine licking the dark,
drinking the clouds

She won't talk about our teenage years
but they still dance behind my eyes
the days when the shadow was eating us
because we were too afraid of the rain,
so afraid that we stayed locked in the basement
where at least the shadows were dependable

Her words were clouds,
billowing from her mouth, twisting around me—
filling my ears with static;
the taste of rain, acidic and sticky,
a humid sweetness entering my lungs . . .
I swallowed the gray for so long

She taught me how to be weak
masquerading it about as honesty
she told me who I was
a definition to squeeze into
shaped from a reflection of herself
she wove me into a stranger

"Freedom sure is sweet"—
the empty words of hope and death that slithered
    from our pens,
as if we couldn't change our fate,
we peeled back our skin and walked about as skeletons.

I remember the Yellow Bird,
here before she came,
the way it sang behind my ribs
like a silver lake within a desert
I left my body behind
dreaming on the staircase
waiting for each yesterday to wave farewell

Those stairs have grown dusty
creases cobwebbed with weary resignation

Yellow bird doesn't come here anymore.

"Hope never abandons you, you abandon it." —*George Weinberg*

Keywords: Fears   Hope   Regrets   Masquerading

The World Needs . . .

by Sierra Ferrier

A pitcher,
So full of emptiness.
Clear water,
Imaginations scramble
Wildly.

Bittersweet aroma
Of small but bulky
Tea bags.
Floating so delicately
Above the water.

The hours pass,
Waiting patiently.
As the sugar strikes
Rock bottom,
Opportunities rise.

The powerful twirl
Of sweetness
Through the bitter tea,
Creates the taste . . .
Of Heaven.

"Tea is drunk to forget the din of the world." —Tien Yiheng

Keywords: Aroma   Sweet   Time   Water

Chicago Newcomer

by Molly Wagener

In a skyscraper sandwich
on Michigan,
I ogled at the framed in sky.
Pristine clear
with scattered white
weightlessness

vanishing
above the glossy windows,
steel rooftops,
and cabs zipping
up and down the asphalt street

This author uses vivid imagery to communicate her impressions of the big city. Note the "skyscraper sandwich," the "glossy windows," and the "steel rooftops." Write a composition in which you describe either a rural or urban environment that impressed you when you saw it for the first time. Use colorful details to bring your description to life.

"A skyscraper is a boast in glass and steel." —*Mason Cooley*

Keywords: Glass   Steel   Automobiles   Street

picket fences

by Laurel Guido

x is like a picket fence, with flowers winding between the wood.

we walked along the sidewalk, fingers intertwined. the warm sun joined us, hidden in our hair and our smiles. his beauty captured by a quick snapshot, a frame of mind. i caught him at the moment he laughed. he was beautiful.

x is like a thunderstorm, dark and mysterious and alive.

we sat against the bricks of my house . . . my blanket was wrapped around us, the edges muddied from the rainwater. tears came quickly from my closed eyes when he told me he would be gone by sunrise.

x is like a breeze, light and fresh in the early morning.

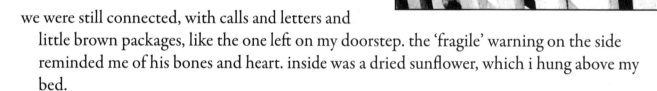

we were still connected, with calls and letters and little brown packages, like the one left on my doorstep. the 'fragile' warning on the side reminded me of his bones and heart. inside was a dried sunflower, which i hung above my bed.

x is like a pulse, strong and splashed with love.

we pressed our aching limbs together, breathing in each other's air. the sun hung low in the trees, haloing his hair and illuminating the relief in his shoulders. we created a rhythm with our hearts, steadily pounding between our lungs.

x is like a dream, colorful and unpredictable and mine.

"A life lived in love will never be dull." —Leo Buscaglia

Keywords: Smile   Love   Sunshine   Laughter

white on white

by Mara Dukats

these are words i've been avoiding for some
    time now
their embers still burn in the ashes of
    memories
where i've tried so many times
to bury them

you see, i've fallen and
not even the shimmer of your cocoa eyes can
    catch me, for
i've landed and it's really not
that harsh
not as gritty as the gravel playground
on a moonless night

i'm shattered on the inside, fragile on
the outside, but strangely whole, you see
i've fallen and i've scraped my knees and
i've an ebbing pain like
shells of empty eggs that spill

no trace of yolks
for yellow is too soft a color
white on white
i've fallen and this time i've got the words
just right i've fallen
out of love

This poet uses images of objects to express her emotions: embers, ashes, gritty gravel, egg shells. Do these images resonate with you? What are some everyday objects you can tie together to convey different feelings?

"If you've broken the eggs, you should make the omelette." —Anthony Eden

Keywords: Fragile   Broken   Fallen   Eggs

Even From a Concrete Sea

by Lila Mackey

Even from a concrete sea,
pushing up from paper waste
in a crush of broken glass,
nearly hidden by the refuse,
half choked by fumes of gas,

Peeks a little greening plant.
Delicate pink petals
spiral in a ruffled dance.

Proof that new beginnings
everywhere are seeking birth
at just the slightest provocation—
a little warmth,
a little water
and a tiny
incidental
piece of earth.

"Almost everything comes from nothing." —*Henri Frédéric Amiel*

Keywords: Survival   Cityscapes   Surprises   Hope

About the Authors

Elizabeth Guy is a mother of four and an avid gardener whose poems have appeared in several publications. A former student at Salem College in Winston-Salem, NC, she has been active in community theater for several years, and she has served as a docent at the Reynolda House Museum of American Art in Winston-Salem. An avid storyteller, she has shared her love of storytelling with thousands of elementary school students over the years. In collaboration with Hank Kellner, she is working on a new collection of poetry and photographs.

Hank Kellner is a veteran of the Korean War and a retired associate professor of English currently based in Winston-Salem. He is the author of *125 Photos for English Composition Classes* (J. Weston Walch, 1978); *How to Be a Better Photographer* (J. Weston Walch, 1980); and, more recently, *Write What You See* (Prufrock Press, 2010). His other writings and photographs have appeared in hundreds of publications nationwide. He is currently developing a new collection of original poetry accompanied by his photographs.